T0115128

DO UNTO OTHERS

JESUS WAS A LIBERAL

BOB SLATE

WestBow
PRESS
A DIVISION OF THOMAS NELSON

Unless otherwise indicated, all Scripture quotations are taken from the Holy Bible, New Living Translation, copyright © 1996, 2004, 2007 by Tyndale House Foundation. Used by permission of Tyndale House Publishers, Inc., Carol Stream, Illinois 60188. All rights reserved.

Author photo and front and back cover photos © 2012 Francine Slate, Slate Photography.
Website: www.slate-photography.com
Facebook: www.facebook.com/capturedbyslatephotography

Back cover photo: A view of the intersection of Broadway and Wall Street in New York City, as seen from Wall Street. When completed in 1846, Trinity Church's neo-Gothic 280-foot spire was the highest point in the city—man's reverential tribute to the glory of God. It is now dwarfed and nearly hidden by towering structures built to the glory of money.

WestBow Press books may be ordered through booksellers or by contacting:

WestBow Press
A Division of Thomas Nelson
1663 Liberty Drive
Bloomington, IN 47403
www.westbowpress.com
1-(866) 928-1240

ISBN: 978-1-4497-5968-1 (sc)
ISBN: 978-1-4497-5967-4 (e)

Library of Congress Control Number: 2012912864

Printed in the United States of America

WestBow Press rev. date: 07/26/2012

For Maryemily

Contents

Foreword by Dave Anderson ix

Do unto Others: Jesus Was a Liberal 1

The Path Beyond 7

Liberalism and God 13

Grace and Economics 23

Social Justice 27

The Woman Caught in Adultery 31

Faith and Freedom Coalition: Wolves in Sheep's Clothing? 37

What Makes Us Human? 45

Constitutional Question: Make Me Pay for My Health Care or
    Make Me Pay for Someone Else's 49

Ground Zero Mosque and Religious Bias 55

Unions and the Demonizing Wedge 61

The Bible and the Constitution 67

Romney: The Sky Is Falling 71

The Problem with Fox News (and MSNBC) 75

Torture and American Exceptionalism 81

Foreword

I t has been said, "There are two things that don't mix-religion and politics." Yet religion and politics are intertwined at every corner of American culture. For politicians and theologians alike, religion can be hijacked for political gain. The polarization of *liberals* and *conservatives* results in trying to paint very difficult social, political, and biblical issues with very narrow brushes. But, as Bob points out, everything is not black and white because "we live in a world with infinite shades of gray."

If you consider yourself a "conservative evangelical Christian," I suspect you might want to ban this book (at least from your local Christian bookstore) based on the title alone. If you are a "yellow dog democrat" you will likely cheer this book without even reading it. I would challenge every Christian to read and consider the underlying message of the book, however.

Bob takes current political hot potatoes such as gay marriage, abortion, and universal health care and essentially asks "What Would Jesus Do?" The answers are not always clear. Nor are they always comfortable.

Using a mix of scripture and sarcasm, Bob will raise the ire of the right-wing political conservative. With sound biblical truth he will also provoke those who do not hold a conservative view of scripture. But his main purpose is not to fan the flames of political rhetoric or religious discourse. His goal is to call those of us who claim the name of Jesus, regardless of our political bent, back to doing what Jesus said to do—"love your neighbor as yourself."

You will not agree with Bob on every point of this book, regardless of which side of the political aisle you sit. By reading it, however, you will be challenged to evaluate your position based on more than a sound bite or a voting guide. After being forced to confront both your politics and your prejudice, you may find that you have common ground with those whose views you oppose based on a position of love and compassion with Jesus at the center.

Dave Anderson
Lead pastor, Crosspoint Community Church
Decatur, Alabama

Do unto Others:
Jesus Was a Liberal

T he title of this book is somewhat misleading, albeit intentionally so. I do not think Jesus was a liberal any more than I think he was politically conservative. But I do believe many of the qualities Jesus demonstrated and promoted—compassion, forgiveness, tolerance for differences, and empathy, for example—are exhibited by today's progressive movement much more than by conservatives.

Characterizations like "liberal" and "conservative" oversimplify complex issues and inaccurately compartmentalize people. Life is not black and white unless one takes an overly superficial view of issues.

We live in a world with infinite shades of gray. Most issues, when they are examined even slightly below the surface, are more complex than the limited palette of black or white can describe. Additionally (with a few exceptions), today's media do little more than scratch the surface of important issues that affect every person. Broad terms like *liberal* and *conservative* allow us to unfairly compartmentalize and demonize others who do not believe exactly as we do without having to dig down to the real issue.

This book's title might lead one to believe it is primarily about politics. That is also misleading. While it deals extensively with political issues, this is not a book about growing a particular party or school of political thought. It is a book about growing the church as a whole. I believe there is no better authority or example for that purpose than Jesus—although the principles he espoused can easily be applied by people of many faiths or by those of no faith at all.

Why, then, does the book dwell on—seem almost obsessed with—politics? There are two reasons for this.

First, it is because politics and government impact people's lives more than almost any other aspect of our society. As Eugene Cho, founder and lead pastor of Quest Church in Seattle, put it in his blog, "I care about politics not because I obsess over politics; rather, politics is important to me because it involves policies, and policies, ultimately, impact people. We have no choice: We must be engaged in our civic responsibilities and affairs."[1]

The other reason this book deals at length with politics is I believe partisan politics (and its divisiveness) is one of the biggest impediments to the growth of God's kingdom on earth today. Many people of other faiths—and those of no faith—observe political activists who call themselves Christians and are turned off. Ralph Reed's groups[2] and Tony Perkins's Family Research Council[3] are but two of many organizations that purport to steer Christians toward the "faith" position on issues, yet even a cursory review of the groups' positions seems to show they reject much of what Jesus taught us about how we should treat those he called "the least of these." The actual purpose of Reed's and Perkins's groups appears to be growing a particular political party. They, like many others, seem intent on misrepresenting progressive thought and perpetuating the belief that God is a Republican.

The media are also guilty of perpetuating the myth that conservatism is the philosophy of people of faith. Any mention of "evangelical Christians" in newspapers or on the television news shows is assumed to be synonymous with "conservatives."

Difference of Degree, Not Absolutes

Most people would agree that the term *conservative* generally describes one who believes in less government, and conversely, *liberal* describes one who believes government has a more prominent role in the lives of citizens.

Conservatives assert, without hesitation, that the more a government is involved, the less liberty its citizens have. Many conservatives take this

---

[1]   Reprinted by Sojourners, www.sojo.net, "Conversation on prayer with President Obama," Feb. 21, 2012.

[2]   Formerly the Christian Coalition, currently the Faith and Freedom Coalition, http://www.ffcoalition.org.

[3]   http://www.frc.org/.

---

for the gospel. It can be exemplified by many of the undeniably attractive quips attributed to former President Ronald Reagan, such as: "The nine most terrifying words in the English language are, 'I'm from the government, and I'm here to help.'"

Reagan made the word *government* a pejorative in the conservative lexicon. Today, conservative commentators like Sean Hannity and Rush Limbaugh need only mention the word to stir up the ire of their followers. Bill O'Reilly sometimes simply dismisses those who disagree with his opinions with the phrase, "That's just liberal thinking."

But where would we be without government? Without the armed forces that defend us from would-be intruders from outside our borders or without the police officers and sheriffs' deputies who protect us from threats initiated within? Without firefighters, teachers, or mail carriers? Without public utility companies that deliver clean water, take away our wastewater, and provide us with electricity and natural gas? Without streets on which to drive?

Further, where would we be without building inspectors and building codes? They protect those of us who know nothing about construction from spending our life savings on a house that will fall down on us in a year or two. Do judges, who settle disputes in matters of law, infringe on our liberty, or do they enable it? Is our liberty restrained by these governmental "intrusions" into our lives, or is our liberty enhanced?

The list of essential government entities goes on and on, but for now let's just consider those listed above and agree that there are some government services that actually enrich our lives. Even at this superficial level, it is apparent that at least some governmental services are crucial. It is not a black-and-white, either/or issue.

Thus, the difference between liberals and conservatives is about the level to which we allow the government to be involved in our lives. It is a difference of degree rather than a difference in absolutes.

Why would I say Jesus was a liberal? Because even though the conservative party in American politics has a near-monopoly on voters who call themselves Christians, I believe that organized conservative Christian thought today—especially on social issues—is pretty much opposed to many of the principles Jesus taught (e.g., giving to the poor, tolerating differences, forgiving rather than judging others).

The messages of the New Testament are many, but chief among these are the good news of God's saving grace through faith in Jesus Christ; our obligation to spread that good news to everyone; and our duty to try to live as Jesus lived. This final goal is a never-ending effort at which we are doomed to fail but for which we are nonetheless obligated to strive.

To try to live as Jesus did requires a thorough examination of his life in context. Failure to recognize this context of the New Testament as a new covenant that overshadows the law of the Old Testament leads to inevitable contradictions in the Bible (an eye for an eye, but offer the other cheek and forgive your transgressor seventy times seven times).

Obviously, Jesus' death on the cross was the ultimate act of generosity, grace, and love, even though none of us deserves it. Jesus was the Lamb of God who sacrificed himself that we might live, even though we fall short.

Because Jesus was and still is God personified, and he knew from the start how his life on earth would end, we must examine all his teachings in this context. Those who disagree with this interpretation are urged to read Hebrews 10.

Matthew 7:12, commonly referred to as the Golden Rule, sums up Jesus' teaching as it applies to our relationships with others: "Do to others whatever you would like them to do to you. This is the essence of all that is taught in the law and the prophets."

"Do unto others . . ." teaches us empathy. It asks us to put ourselves into another's position and consider how we would like to be treated if the shoe were on the other foot. It is an admonishment to act always out of love for others.

First John 4:20-21 puts it another way: "If anyone says, 'I love God,' yet hates his brother, he is a liar. For anyone who does not love his brother, whom he has seen, cannot love God, whom he has not seen. And he has given us this command: Whoever loves God must also love his brother."

During the Republican presidential primary debate in South Carolina on January 16, 2012, US Rep. Ron Paul, a GOP candidate, called for the United States to adopt the Golden Rule in foreign policy matters.

"My point is that if another country does to us what we do to others, we aren't going to like it very much. So I would say maybe we ought to consider a golden rule in foreign policy," said Paul, at the time the only military veteran left in the GOP field. "We endlessly bomb these other countries and then we wonder why they get upset with us."

Sadly, boos and jeers from the Republican crowd drowned out most of Paul's observation. The GOP base, which proudly wears its Christianity on its sleeve, openly booed a call to obey the Golden Rule.

Has partisan politics become more important than Jesus?

Tolerance is intolerable for the modern conservative movement, yet Jesus taught us to love our neighbors, love our enemies, and forgive others "seventy times seven" times. He taught us to turn the other cheek. He hung out with lowly fishermen, corrupt tax collectors, and sinners of every stripe. He showed kindness and compassion to adulterers and others who were among the lost. He healed the sick and gave succor to the poor. He told us that what we did for "the least of these," we did for him.

Do these acts seem to exemplify the policy positions of today's conservative movement? Are we tolerant of Muslims, for example, or homosexuals? Do we value the lives of "the least of these"?

Why did Jesus teach empathy and tolerance? Why did he constantly remind us to love rather than to judge others?

First, he did it because it is the right thing—the godly thing. It is the way and life Jesus referred to when he said, "I am the way and the truth and the life. No one comes to the father except through me" (John 14:6). It is the example of grace he showed when he allowed himself to be tortured and killed for our sakes, even though we did not deserve it.

Second, people are much more likely to accept your philosophy if you show them love and compassion rather than hate or condemnation. Would the woman caught in adultery have gone and sinned no more had Jesus urged the teachers of religious law and the Pharisees to stone her? (No, in fact Jesus turned the tables and forced them to examine their own lives; to put themselves in her place; to practice empathy.) Would the sick, the lame, and the blind have been converted had Jesus refused to heal their ills? Would the thief on the cross next to him have been converted had Jesus condemned rather than forgiven him?

Take many of the most divisive social issues today (abortion, same-sex relationships, government assistance to the poor, universal health care, capital punishment, government regulation, tolerance of other faiths, torture of prisoners, prayer in school, war versus diplomacy) and consider the conservative position. Then ask: Is that the position of love, of grace, of empathy? Is that the same position I would take if the shoe were on the other foot?

I am not saying ours is a Christian nation (although the vast majority of Americans consider themselves Christians). This is yet another nuanced distinction that requires more than a cursory examination of the surface. I believe there is strength in the concept of separation of church and state. Our founders came here to escape the tyranny of the British, including the

Church of England. People of all faiths and those of no faith have the right to be free from the government (or the majority of voters) telling them when to pray and what to believe.

No political party in America has a monopoly on God. Many people who consider themselves Christians are not easily compartmentalized as either liberals or conservatives.

Most of us form our political views based on our larger worldview. Many of us form our worldviews based on God's Word. This book attempts to take one man's interpretation of the good news and apply it to the rough-and-tumble political landscape, where truth and the welfare of the American people are often trumped by political expediency.

The Path Beyond

*The best way to align your will to God's is not to
subordinate your desires to others' needs, but to make
meeting others' needs your exact desire.*

In one popular analogy, Jesus the Savior is represented as a bridge spanning a canyon from the state of being lost to a state of salvation. In the context of Old Testament law and tradition, Jesus is the subsequent blood sacrifice God required to shed his grace on every man, woman, and child who earnestly repents and seeks to cross the chasm between life on this earth and eternal life in heaven. We do not earn the right to cross the bridge; there is no fare we can pay. Jesus paid the fare for all of us.

I believe that, too often, the modern Christian church focuses only on that bridge and ignores the path that necessarily follows beyond. That path beyond, or "second bridge," is what Jesus was describing when he said, "I am the way, the truth, and the life. No one can come to the Father except through me" (John 14:6).

Jesus called himself the *way,* the *truth,* and the *life.* He was telling the disciples he was, and still is, the way to eternal life with God. And yes, there is power in Jesus' name we can only begin to comprehend (see John 14:13-14). But calling on Jesus' name is not the only truth he taught. Calling on Jesus' name is the first step—the first bridge—in a transformative process that continues throughout the rest of our lives.

Too often, I believe, people see God's grace through faith in Jesus as a means to get themselves across the chasm, but then fail to continue down the path that was Jesus' *way.* Could this be the result of a fault in the Church; an overemphasis on the bridge and a comparative disregard for the hard work that continuing along the path beyond requires? Is it an appeal to selfishness when selflessness is actually the key?

The path beyond is the way, the truth, and the life. Yes, it is to "go and make disciples of all the nations . . ." (Matt. 28:19), but it is also to "teach these new disciples to obey all the commands I have given you" (Matt. 28:20). Those commands are loving God, loving our neighbors as ourselves, loving our enemies, seeking God's will and making it our own, and being the hands and feet of Jesus, not just so others will see Jesus in us, but also because it is the example he lived (see Phil. 2:5-11). In other words, the way, the truth, and the life is to humble ourselves as Jesus did—to serve our fellow man; to become other-focused rather than self-absorbed.

If we become too focused on the bridge and don't also teach about the path beyond, we make the church into a field filled with weeds and rocks. The seeds we sow do not bear fruit but get choked out. Too often today, those on the outside perceive the church as an example of hate and judgment. Many Christians assume this is a fault of those outside the church. I believe it is the result of a failure by many of us to convey our concern for others. For many within the church, Christianity is an excuse for us to feel superior to others as members of an exclusive club rather than an opportunity—even an obligation—to put others' interests before our own. Could this be the result of us trying to *scare* people into heaven but neglecting to teach them how to navigate the path beyond and thus denying them the essential, transformational gift of the Holy Spirit?

In other words: If we are bringing people to Jesus by appealing to their selfish interests—showing them how to avoid an eternity in hell—but not also preaching sincere repentance and transformation motivated by love of others, then we are not really bringing people to Jesus at all. And the results are evident in a lack of fruit—love, joy, peace, patience, kindness, goodness, faithfulness, gentleness, and self-control (Gal. 5:22-23).

In Luke 8:18, Jesus said: "So pay attention to how you hear. To those who listen to my teaching, more understanding will be given. But for those who are not listening, even what they think they understand will be taken away from them." Listen! This is a great promise, but it is also a frightening prospect. How we hear the word is the difference between gaining everything and losing everything. Are we listening?

When the church focuses solely on saving the lost from hell without demanding a total submission and transformation to selflessness from selfishness, it does a disservice God's kingdom on earth. When the church fails to teach both the bridge *and* the path beyond, it perpetuates an institution that is far from the church that Jesus came here to establish.

We need to show the world why, exactly, the way and the truth and the life—a focus on others, a willingness to humble ourselves as Jesus did—are superior to a life spent perpetuating our own selfish interests.

Second Corinthians 5:15: "[Christ] died for everyone so that those who receive his new life will no longer live for themselves."

In summary: Too often, we, as the church, view faith in and a saving knowledge of Jesus Christ as the finish line, when in reality, Jesus said it was just the start.

Belief Is Not Enough

Jesus is real, he is of the Trinity (all three, one), and he was God come to earth in human form to be a blood sacrifice for our sins. It was the single greatest act of love ever performed. We do not deserve it. It is only through God's grace that we receive this gift.

Yes, Jesus *is* the way, the truth, and the life. No one comes to the Father except through him.

But to simply believe this is not enough. Demons believe this. Even Satan believes. To confess is the first step, but it is not enough. One must be *transformed*.

In his book, *Love Wins: A Book About Heaven, Hell and the Fate of Every Person Who Ever Lived*, Rob Bell considers this dilemma in the church.[4]

Bell discusses the various ways different denominations believe one may get to heaven, such as saying a prayer at some point in his or her life, performing a specific rite or ritual, taking a class, being baptized, joining a church, or having something happen somewhere, at some time, in his or her heart.

"That, of course, raises more questions," Bell writes. "What about the people who have said some form of 'the prayer' at some point in their lives, but it means nothing to them today? What about those who said it in a highly emotionally charged environment like a youth camp or church service because it was the thing to do, but were unaware of the significance of what

---

4   Rob Bell, *Love Wins: A Book About Heaven, Hell and the Fate of Every Person Who Ever Lived.* Harper Collins, 2011.

they were doing? *What about people who have never said the prayer and don't claim to be Christians, but live a more Christlike life than some Christians?"* (My emphasis)[5]

Bell's point is: There must be more to living a Christian life than getting somewhere else.

"If that's the gospel, the good news—if what Jesus does is get people somewhere else—then the central message of the Christian faith has very little to do with this life other than getting you what you need for the next one."[6]

"Which leads to a far more disturbing question," Bell continues. "So is it true that the kind of person you are doesn't ultimately matter, as long as you've said or prayed or believed the right things? If you truly believed that, and you were surrounded by Christians who believed that, then you wouldn't have much motivation to do anything about the present suffering in the world, because you would believe you were going to leave someday and go *somewhere else* to be with Jesus. If this understanding of the good news of Jesus prevailed among Christians, the belief that Jesus' message is about how to get somewhere else, *you could possibly end up with a world in which millions of people were starving, thirsty, and poor; the earth was being exploited and polluted; disease and despair were everywhere; and Christians weren't known for doing much about it. If it got bad enough, you might even have people rejecting Jesus because of how his followers lived."* (My emphasis)

"That would be tragic."[7]

The gospel is much better than that. It is more than a ticket to get somewhere else.

When Jesus said, "I am the way . . ." he was saying he was showing us *how to live.* Simply calling on his name, without being truly transformed, is not enough.

James 2:14: "What good is it, dear brothers and sisters, if you say you have faith but don't show it by your actions?"

Galatians 5:6 "For when we place our faith in Christ Jesus, there is no benefit in being circumcised or being uncircumcised. What is important is faith expressing itself in love."

In other words, it is not the act of profession that is most important, but it is the relationship that follows, and the fruit of that relationship consists of the acts resulting from our *transformation.*

---

[5] Ibid., p. 9
[6] Ibid.
[7] Ibid.

So how are we to live? Jesus showed us, and it can be generally summed up in four words: love God, love others (Matt. 22:37-40). In other words, "Do to others whatever you would like them to do to you. This is the essence of all that is taught in the law and the prophets" (Matt. 7:12).

Who are we to love? All others—not just those who look like us, act as we act, and believe as we believe. We are to love even our enemies. Just because we accepted an undeserved gift does not make us any better than someone else. Have we forgotten that we were all, at one point, someone else?

James 4:11-12: "Don't speak evil against each other, dear brothers and sisters. If you criticize and judge each other, then you are criticizing and judging God's law. But your job is to obey the law, not to judge whether it applies to you. God alone, who gave the law, is the Judge. He alone has the power to save or to destroy. So what right do you have to judge your neighbor?" In other words, quit focusing solely on the bridge and pay more attention to the path beyond. Otherwise, you're stuck in one place.

Galatians 5:22-23: "But the Holy Spirit produces this kind of fruit in our lives: love, joy, peace, patience, kindness, goodness, faithfulness, gentleness, and self-control."

Here is a test: Do others, especially non-believers, know we are Christians by our love?

If many Christians would quit thinking only about themselves and begin to focus on others' interests, as Jesus taught, the rest of the world would sit up and pay closer attention and maybe even be transformed. Let's be the hands and feet of Jesus—not an exclusive club that admits only others who act, think, and look just like us and rejects those who don't.

After all, Jesus came to seek and save that which was lost (Luke 19:1-10). As Dennis Pethers put it: "People who call themselves God-loving people are only God-loving people if they love the people God loves."[8]

Paul put it this way in his letter to the Romans:

"Don't think you are better than you really are. Be honest in your evaluation of yourselves, measuring yourselves by the faith God has given us.... Don't just pretend to love others. Really love them ... Live in harmony with each other. Don't be too proud to enjoy the company of ordinary people. And don't think you know it all!" (Rom. 12:3, 9, 16)

---

[8]   Dennis Pethers, The Sticks conference, Nov. 10, 2010.

Liberalism and God

O ne problem with the faith-and-politics connection is the intention of some conservatives to misrepresent progressive thought and stake a claim that God is a Republican.

On June 24, 2011, while speaking on the radio with Family Research Council President Tony Perkins, US Rep. Todd Akin, R-Missouri, said, "Well, I think NBC has a long record of being very liberal and *at the heart of liberalism really is a hatred for God and a belief that government should replace God.*" (My emphasis)[9]

Akin was seeking the GOP nomination to run for the US Senate seat then held by Claire McCaskill, D-Missouri. After a public outcry by some in the faith community, Akin later clarified his comment by saying that he was making reference to discussions of God in the public square—not to individuals' relationships with the creator.

But, of course, by the time Akin issued his clarification, the damage had already been done.

The Rev. Krista Taves of Emerson Unitarian Universalist Chapel in Ellisville, Missouri, said Akin's comment "shows how very little he knows about liberals and how very little he knows about God."[10]

---

[9]   Colby Hochmuth, June 28, 2011, "Lawmaker apologizes for liberal 'hatred of God' quip," Fox News

[10]   Jason Hancock, June 29, 2011, "Akin changes course, apologizes for comment," St. Louis Post-Dispatch

"I'm a liberal because I love God and all God's creation," Taves said. "I value equality, fairness, and compassionate justice because my faith informs my politics."

Akin is just one of many examples of conservative politicians claiming the endorsement of God.

And the problem is that those politicians' target audience often does not know or care if their candidate misrepresents the truth.

A more recent example: televangelist Pat Robertson on Jan. 3, 2012—as Iowans were heading to their caucuses to select the Republican candidate for president of the United States—told his viewers that God had revealed to him who the next president would be.[11] Robertson said he wasn't supposed to reveal that identity, "So I'll leave you in the dark." But, not surprisingly, God told Robertson that he is no fan of Barack Obama and that the current president is the cause of future economic collapse.

"I'm going to read just as I wrote down, as if I'm hearing from the Lord these words," Robertson said. He shared that the "country was disintegrating, and to expect chaos and paralysis."

"Your country will be torn apart by internal stress, a house divided cannot stand. Your president holds a radical view of the direction of your country which is at odds with the majority," Robertson said, reading from the notes he had taken in his discussion with God. "Your president holds a view that is at odds with the majority; it's a radical view of the future of this country, so that's why we're having this division."

Robertson says he asked God about future hardships, including an electromagnetic pulse, solar radiation, Mayan galaxy alignment, nuclear threats from North Korea or Iran, an earthquake, a volcano, and a power failure. Each time, God denied that those factors would contribute to the disintegration of the country.

"It's an economic collapse," Robertson said. "And God said, and I quote, 'This is not my judgment; they are bringing it upon themselves.'"

School Prayer
Another perplexing example of the faith—government disconnect is the myth, perpetuated by some on the right, that children are not allowed to

---

[11]   http://www.christianpost.com/news/god-reveals-to-pat-robertson-the-next-us-president-66312/

pray or read their Bibles in public schools because of objections by liberal groups like the American Civil Liberties Union.

One would think that conservative Christians would be eager to let their children know that student-initiated prayer and non-compulsory Bible study (and even evangelizing) are legal, acceptable acts as long as they don't disrupt the school routine. Instead, most Americans believe the myth that such acts are prohibited.

Case law is fairly settled on this First Amendment issue, although legitimate disputes occasionally arise over what constitutes school endorsement of religion. While public schools, as government agencies, cannot force students to pray or study any particular religious document (under the establishment clause), neither can they prohibit students from doing so (under the free exercise clause).

While many on the right would have the public believe the ACLU seeks to make the United States a godless nation, the organization is, in fact, protecting First Amendment rights of all Americans—those of diverse faiths as well as those of no faith.

Those Christians who are outraged by prohibitions of state-endorsed prayer often fail to recognize the protection they receive from the First Amendment establishment clause. Do they really want the government to endorse one particular faith; to tell us what to believe and how to pray and to whom? Most would answer with a resounding "no." Those who answer in the affirmative always have a preference for which particular set of beliefs they want the government to endorse: "Mine."

Weiss v. District Board (1890), one of the first high-profile disputes to set a precedent, sometimes called The Edgerton Bible case, was actually initiated by a Christian (Catholic) group that objected to the use of the King James Bible in Wisconsin public schools.

Most of the more recent school-prayer cases have arisen over disputes involving the use of public facilities or equipment, like public-address systems, to accommodate group prayer. Those on the Christian right are often outraged at such prohibitions. But how would they feel if those facilities were used to promote Islamic tenets, to compel praise for Hindu deities, or to indoctrinate their children to the rites of the Man-Boy Love Society?

Texas Gov. Rick Perry, when he was seeking the Republican presidential nomination in 2012, ran a television ad in which he said, "[T]here's something wrong in this country when gays can serve openly in the military but our kids can't openly celebrate Christmas or pray in school." Perry's conclusion might be right if his premises were not false.

In spite of the rhetoric, there is no war on Christmas. Kids may pray in school.

Fellow GOP candidate Newt Gingrich, in December 2011, went so far as to propose presidential powers to eliminate some federal courts, to arrest and replace what he calls "activist judges," and to ignore some Supreme Court rulings. When proposing this major shift in the constitutional balance of powers, Gingrich cited a misguided lower-court decision (quickly overturned) that prohibited a school superintendent from using the word "benediction" at a graduation ceremony.

One wonders, however, how Gingrich would feel about a benediction at graduation that included the words "Allahu Akbar."

Why do Christian conservatives not focus on the protections First Amendment rulings provide them and their children? Why do we emphasize and publicize the prohibitions and spread the myth that our children cannot pray or read the Bible or evangelize in public schools?

Could it be that the political advantage obtained by being perceived as a martyred, victimized group trumps the world-changing, kingdom-building good that can be done by exercising our rights?

The government must walk a fine line between the prohibitions of the establishment clause and the accommodations of the free exercise clause, and schools and other taxpayer-funded entities generally do a good job when they follow the direction of court precedent.

Problems invariably arise when governments—often overzealous school boards or other elected officials with good intentions—overstep their discretion.

Former Alabama Supreme Court Chief Justice Roy Moore is one example of a government official who went too far.

From the date of his appointment as a circuit judge, Moore, a Republican, opened court with prayer and displayed a small plaque containing the Ten Commandments in his courtroom. Higher courts eventually ruled the practice of prayer and the display of the Ten Commandments were violations of the establishment clause. This gave Moore a political issue he would ride all the way to election to the top of the state's high court.

And when he became chief justice, Moore used taxpayer dollars to construct a 5,200-pound granite Ten Commandments monument and place it in the central rotunda of the state judicial building.

He later defied a federal court order by refusing to remove the monument. He was eventually removed from office.

Judge Moore had every right to build such a monument (although not with tax dollars) and display it on private property. Why, then, did he choose to blatantly defy the law and a court order? His deep religious convictions, some might argue. Or political expediency. Demagoguery. Pandering.

Judge Moore later wrote a column for WorldNet Daily, published Dec. 13, 2006, expressing his opinion that Keith Ellison, a Muslim elected to Congress by the voters in Minnesota, could not honestly take the oath of office and should therefore be barred from taking office. Moore cited as his reasoning his belief that the Quran denies all religions but Islam.[12]

One need only use the "Do unto others . . ." principle—the principle of empathy—to see the hypocrisy of Moore's position. The irony is that Moore's version of Christianity denies religious freedom to anyone whose beliefs differ from his own.

US Rep. Michele Bachmann, R-Minnesota, is also expert at flouting her conservative credentials and insisting God is on her side. Bachmann sought the GOP nomination in the 2012 presidential race before eventually suspending her campaign. She regularly misrepresents the positions of the Obama administration. During the GOP primary race, however, she also targeted Republican front-runner Mitt Romney's position on legalized abortion.

Pro-life *and* Pro-choice

Bachmann is a smart woman. Surely, she realizes that the abortion issue is complex and nuanced and that politicians can be pro-life while endorsing a public-policy position that allows women to make their own medical decisions without government interference. But in her public comments about Romney, Bachmann painted the issue as black and white.

It is yet another example of a conservative politician claiming the endorsement of God.

Conservatives and some extreme liberals would have you believe the abortion issue is black and white. But characterizing the issue as either/or, pro-life or pro-choice, again oversimplifies one of the most complex, polarizing, and mischaracterized issues our society faces today.

---

[12]   Judge Roy Moore, "Muslim Ellison Should Not Sit in Congress," *WorldNet Daily*, December 13, 2006, www.wnd.com/2006/12/39271/.

Most Americans are pro-choice by definition and many don't even realize it. A majority of Americans are pro-life and anti-abortion by practice, but also pro-choice by policy. In other words, they think in almost all cases abortion is the wrong decision, but it should be a decision made by the mother—not the government—with options other than a shady character in a back alley with a coat hanger and a vacuum hose.

Politically, the Republican Party has owned this issue for years by oversimplifying and couching it in the simplest of terms. If you are not pro-life by the party definition, you advocate the slaughter of millions of innocent, unborn lives. You are a "baby-killer" in the language used by US Rep. Randy Neugebauer as he shouted "baby-killer" on March 21, 2010, during the historic health-care reform debate in the House of Representatives.

Similarly, many conservatives characterize President Barack Obama as a baby-killer because he believes the government should stay out of what is usually the most difficult decision a woman must ever make. Baby-killer: as if Obama himself were performing the procedure.

President Obama recognizes that the Supreme Court decision in Roe v. Wade, which recognized a woman's right to decide what to do with her body but also drew lines on when during the pregnancy a woman could no longer turn back, is the law of the land. The Supreme Court faced the difficult, if not impossible, task of drawing a line. It did so reasonably. Barack Obama did not decide Roe v. Wade any more than Ronald Reagan did.

In reality, every situation in which a woman considers terminating her pregnancy, for whatever reason, is a tragedy. But some reasons merit consideration, such as a threat to the life of the mother, or perhaps rape or incest. Again, shades of gray.

But the black-and-white rhetoric is thrown against the wall and much of it sticks. In truth, the "socialist" Obama is for less government intervention on this issue than conservatives, who in this instance favor government regulation of medical decisions. Go figure.

As President Bill Clinton said, abortions should be legal, safe, and rare. Rare is the key word.

Setting aside for a moment the fact that abortions will be performed whether legal or outlawed, let's look at God's law.

God commands us to love him. But does he force us to love him, or are we saved by his grace through our faith? In other words, does God give us a choice when it comes to the most important decision a person can make, a decision that affects him or her eternally?

When it comes to questions with eternal consequences, God is pro-choice.

Hey, Wait a Minute!

Do you see what I did there? I framed the discussion in such a way as to be able to argue God was on one side. And that is what happens way too often in political discussions.

Of course, the topic was not eternal salvation through Jesus Christ. The topic was abortion.

And unless we are willing to get down in the weeds and discuss the details of the real issue, we will never be able to find any common ground or understand how someone can be on the other side. Abortion is too tragic a circumstance and too complex an issue for a bumper-sticker answer. (In fact, the "Choose Life" license plates available in many states actually espouse the pro-choice position because, for a woman to choose life, she must first be afforded a choice.)

Let's start by acknowledging that all folks who are pro-choice are not necessarily pro-abortion. Just because abortion is legal does not mean women must elect the procedure. The United States never has forced and never will force a woman to have an abortion.

Conversely, making abortion illegal would not prevent all abortions.

Yet, nearly every day on conservative radio and television, and in right-leaning publications, politicians who oppose government intervention on the issue are misleadingly portrayed as "abortion supporters."

A headline in the May 3, 2012, Washington Examiner, for example: "Carter, Democrats press Obama to junk abortion support" portrays Obama as pro-abortion, when that is a misrepresentation of his position.

Just a week earlier, Republican Mississippi Gov. Phil Bryant went a step further when he said on an Internet talk show that pro-choice advocates' "one mission in life is to abort children, is to kill children in the womb."[13]

It is reasonable to disagree on issues—especially ones as important and heart-wrenching as abortion rights. But we will never reach a consensus when we are framing the discussion in lies rather than reality.

Let's also acknowledge that abortion terminates a potential person. So it is certainly a heavy, difficult issue.

---

[13]   "Gov. Phil Bryant discusses new abortion law and its opponents," Jackson Clarion-Ledger, April 25, 2012.

Is abortion murder?

To answer that question, one must attempt to determine exactly when life begins. When Pastor Rick Warren asked then-candidate Barack Obama, at Saddleback Church during the 2008 presidential race, when life begins, Sen. Obama replied that the answer was above his pay grade.

Obama took a lot of criticism for that answer, especially from those who frame the discussion in a manner to suit their political advantage.

But the question is not easily answered. There is disagreement—even among those who believe that life is a sacred gift from God. While the official Catholic position is that life begins at conception, others believe life begins later—or earlier. Does life begin only at birth? When the child can survive independently of the mother? Or when the child has a sense of identity or self? These are difficult questions not easily answered by scientists or physicians, let alone laypersons.

Some states have adopted "personhood" laws that establish life legally begins at conception. In other states, similar efforts have failed. And still other states have tried to establish that life actually begins prior to conception, in an unfertilized egg.

In addition to the viability of the prenatal life, the health of the mother must also be considered. If the fetus threatens the mother's life due to complications, which life takes priority? If left up to the mother, many would certainly choose to save their own lives. Others, I suspect, would sacrifice themselves for the sake of their unborn child. But isn't that a decision the woman should make?

With so many different opinions, everyone wants his own belief to be the law of the land.

That is why I say above that the Supreme Court, in Roe v. Wade, decided reasonably. We can argue about the existence or absence of a constitutional right to privacy or about whether the federal government may make medical decisions for women. In Roe v. Wade, the Court said a woman has a right to choose only during the first trimester of pregnancy. It was a compromise based on common sense and the best science available at the time.

What would happen if pro-life advocates (including those who are pro-choice) spent their time and efforts actually attempting to make abortions rare rather than focusing on the law or misrepresenting and demonizing others' positions? What if they spent their energy trying to change lives instead of trying to change the law? What if their efforts were focused on persuading women in heartbreaking circumstances to carry their children?

What if they signed up to adopt an unwanted child? What if they volunteered at crisis pregnancy centers?

What if they sat down with pro-choice advocates and had an actual discussion?

There are also those on the far left that take the issue too far and misrepresent the position of pro-life advocates. There really is no *war on women*. And abortion should never be a *convenience*.

Instead of focusing on the extremes or demonizing the "other," what if folks put themselves in the other person's shoes?

As far as the statement above, "When it comes to questions with eternal consequences, God is pro-choice," is concerned, that, too, can be debated. We can discuss free will versus predestination and determinism, and we can discuss whether the ideas are compatible. We can discuss Calvin and Luther, Augustine and Aquinas, moral agency and conscience.

These are concepts and ideas difficult to reconcile. The answer is way above my pay grade.

But whatever one believes must, at the end of the day, be taken on faith.

Grace and Economics

Many of us base our worldview on the gospel. Our politics must be formed consistently with our worldview. Thus, while I am a staunch proponent of separation of church and state, I nonetheless act in a manner consistent with my beliefs (and respect others' rights to do the same).

Grace is the means by which something of value may be given to a recipient even though the recipient does not deserve it. It is a concept that can be applied to secular situations as well.

In my opinion (and it's only that) the world would be a better place if more people were willing to exhibit grace instead of worrying about what others deserve. I do not believe we must demean or deprive others in order to climb our own ladder of prosperity. If we would all work for the betterment of everyone else, what a wonderful world this could be.

In fact, our capitalistic democratic republic depends on everyone's prosperity.

Fact: A 2011 study by University of California-Berkeley economists shows that the share of total American income going to the top 1 percent of households rose to 19.8 percent in 2010.

I keep reading about the top five percent of American earners who pay 25 percent of the income taxes collected (but those articles don't mention that they make 55 percent of the income or that the richest 10 percent controls two-thirds of all wealth) and the 47 percent of the country who "contribute nothing."

First, nobody in America "contributes nothing." Anyone who buys food or a car or even a stick of chewing gum pays taxes—and contributes to the free-market economy.

Second, the latest statistics show that more than forty-six million Americans now live in poverty. That should make everyone at least uncomfortable, if not downright angry.

So-called conservatives often misrepresent so-called liberals' position on income disparity by characterizing it as *socialism* and *class warfare*. The 99 percent of Americans (financially) are envious of the top one percent, they say. Liberals hate the rich. When Barack Obama advocated *spreading the wealth around* during the 2008 presidential election campaign, Samuel Joseph Wurzelbacher (a.k.a. Joe the Plumber), John McCain, and Sarah Palin insisted Obama was a socialist. That misrepresentation remains popular today among many conservatives.

This is more black-and-white thinking.

We often hear conservatives talk about the lazy poor. And there are actually some lazy poor in America (even some lazy rich). But half the country? Unemployment was at 8.5 percent in December 2011, not 50 percent. Does the term *lazy poor* apply to those who work two jobs and still can't afford to feed their families and heat their homes?

The United States ranks seventy-eighth in the world in income disparity between the upper and lower quintiles, behind countries like India, Vietnam, Indonesia, and Kenya, according to data in the Human Development Report 2007-2008 from the United Nations Development Program.

Is this a people problem or a systemic problem?

Newt Gingrich recently said many poor children have no work ethic because they have no role models who have to "show up (for work) on Monday." He suggested child labor laws "are truly stupid" and specifically suggested that poor children should be paid to work as janitors in their schools.

Gingrich said, "Core policies of protecting unionization and bureaucratization against children . . . has [sic] done more to create income inequality in the United States than any other single policy."

It is true that many successful Americans started out with a newspaper delivery route, a lemonade stand, or a similar entrepreneurial endeavor as a pre-teen. Learning a work ethic at an early age is a good thing. But having young, poor children clean toilets at their schools does not seem to be the appropriate response.

It is also true that many successful Americans started out with millions of dollars of inherited wealth.

Progressives do not seek equality. They seek equal opportunity—or at least as level a playing field as possible.

Our free-market economy works best when everyone has the means to acquire necessities. When the poorest of the poor are able to obtain goods and services, those who provide those goods and services benefit from their patronage.

Similarly, progressives do not believe being rich is inherently evil, as many conservatives would have you believe. Progressives do believe, however, in *social justice:* the concept that all human beings have value and basic human rights. How can we justify corporate chief executives making tens (or hundreds) of millions of dollars annually when some front-line workers for the same company live below the poverty line?

Progressives do not begrudge CEOs and others their successes. Progressives believe, first, that those who work hard and contribute to society deserve compensation to support (at least) a comfortable lifestyle, and second, that those who derive the most benefit from society (in the form of higher wages) can afford to pay a larger share of the taxes required to sustain the country.

Society has an obligation to provide not equality, but equal opportunity.

The free market is, in fact, the best system devised for rewarding hard work and punishing sloth. But, as with any political philosophy, unbridled purity ignores reality.

Progressives like those in the Occupy movement demand a system that promotes fairness, not one that creates incentives for unethical behavior and rewards those who abuse it for personal gain at the expense of others.

To claim the free market needs no regulation, or can't be improved by opportunities that are more equitable, is to distort reality.

Supply-siders tend to ignore the need for demand in order for markets to operate.

Good luck to those wealthy titans of business when the poor 50 percent who *contribute nothing* (except the largest percentage of their income on necessities like food, shelter, and health care) disappear, along with their markets for goods and services.

When will the far right acknowledge that a prosperous middle and lower class is a prerequisite for a prosperous upper class? Isn't it obvious?

Social Justice

Many of my conservative friends insist charity is the responsibility of individuals—not the "confiscatory government who takes my money at gunpoint."

Wow.

And those same friends insist that government-assistance programs are really designed to keep the poor downtrodden (for political expediency).

Double wow.

First, if taking care of "the least of these" (Matt. 25:40, 45) is solely the responsibility of private individuals, then most of us are doomed to eternal punishment (v. 46). A larger percentage of Americans now lives below the poverty line than at any time in our country's history. As individuals, we are clearly failing when it comes to fulfilling our biblical charitable obligations.

Jesus taught us to love others. If it is not only okay, but the right thing—a moral imperative—for *people* to help the less fortunate, then why is it not also the right thing for a government *of the people, by the people,* and *for the people* to help the less fortunate as well? Is it exempt from this obligation simply because it is the government? I do not read anywhere in the Bible where Jesus said "love others—unless you are the government."

"But government is always more inefficient than the private sector," my conservative friends say. The problem is with the word "always": There are *always* exceptions.

I am certainly a strong proponent of separation of church and state—I don't want government telling me how, when, or where to worship. But there is nothing in the constitutional concept of separation, nor anything in the Bible, that prohibits God's people and the government from *both* trying to achieve the goals Jesus espoused. In fact, some public-private partnerships have been quite successful in solving problems like access to drinking water and health care. Most road building today is a public-private venture. It is doubtful the railroads would have been built without participation by both government and private ventures.

While there are those who object to government's *confiscatory* practice of providing assistance to the neediest individuals ("the least of these"), there are also others who object to the government's use of tax dollars to kill innocent civilians in Iraq, Afghanistan, and elsewhere.

I ask my conservative Christian friends to think carefully before answering which of these two government activities is more objectionable: assisting the needy or killing innocents abroad?

"Every gun that is made," President Dwight D. Eisenhower told his listeners in an April 16, 1953, speech to the American Society of Newspaper Editors, "every warship launched, every rocket fired signifies, in the final sense, a theft from those who hunger and are not fed, those who are cold and are not clothed."

Any nation that pours its treasure into the purchase of armaments is spending more than mere money, the president said.

"It is spending the sweat of its laborers, the genius of its scientists, the hopes of its children. The cost of one modern heavy bomber is this: a modern brick school in more than thirty cities. It is two electric power plants, each serving a town of sixty-thousand population. It is two fine, fully equipped hospitals. It is some fifty miles of concrete pavement. We pay for a single fighter plane with a half-million bushels of wheat. We pay for a single destroyer with new homes that could have housed more than eight thousand people. This is, I repeat, the best way of life to be found on the road the world has been taking. This is not a way of life at all in any sense. Under the cloud of threatening war, it is humanity hanging from a cross of iron."

Eisenhower knew government is limited in resources and must therefore prioritize spending programs. And for Eisenhower, who had been the supreme commander of Allied forces in Europe during World War II, the choice between guns and butter was a no-brainer.

What Would Jesus Cut?

In the 1990s, Christian leaders developed a catchphrase to sum up, concisely yet accurately, the concept of following Jesus as we make choices in our daily lives. The "What Would Jesus Do?" movement encouraged followers to ask themselves that same simple question to help make decisions, and then to behave accordingly in their acts and words.

While simple linguistically, the WWJD concept is rooted in deep theological thought. If we truly want to do God's will, we must put aside our selfish desires and make choices based on the life and teaching of Jesus. (See Phil. 2:5)

Ideally, our lives change as our own desires align with God's will. We make choices not just because we know them to be what's right, but because, as we grow spiritually, what we want actually becomes identical to what God wants us to do.

The rub, of course, is to know what God wants us to do.

Knowing and recognizing God's will comes from studying scripture—especially studying the words and acts of Jesus—and communicating with God on a daily basis through prayer. Prayer is not just asking for things we want; listening to the Holy Spirit is key to true communication with God.

God's will and Jesus' life and teaching can be summed up as putting others' well-being ahead of our own; to do for "the least of these"; to do unto others as we would have them do unto us; to love our neighbors as ourselves.

In other words:

> The best way to align my will to God's is
> not to subordinate my desires to others'
> needs, but to make meeting others' needs
> my exact desire.

Do you get the distinction there? We do the right thing not just because we know it's what we *should* do, but because it's what we actually *want* to do.

In 2010, a community of believers calling itself Sojourners (www.sojo.net) resurrected the WWJD fad and applied it to public policy and budgeting. Like Eisenhower's "guns and butter" choice, the "What Would Jesus Cut?" campaign challenged lawmakers to be conscious of how their policies and legislation affect others—especially the poor and vulnerable, since those were the people about whom Jesus taught us to be concerned.

Some who misunderstood the WWJC movement's intent attacked it as heresy. But the WWJC effort was not an attempt to transform the Sermon on the Mount into legislation; it was, rather, an effort to ensure that Christian lawmakers weigh the interests of and consequences for the powerless when faced with setting public policy priorities and making legislative decisions.

WWJC is not a fad or a heretical movement. It is an attempt to represent the interests of the powerless and poor amid the constant lobbying by corporate interests and defense contractors when considering public policy decisions and their effect on the public.

While democracy depends on individuals expressing and acting on their own interests, it can be transformed into something even greater when others' well-being becomes our primary concern.

Some who call themselves Christians not only fail to see the potential positive impact cooperation between faith-based and secular groups can achieve, they preach against it. In doing so, they preach against the gospel as revealed in God's word and exemplified by Jesus' life.

The Woman Caught in Adultery

I n this familiar story from John 8:1-11, the teachers of religious law and Pharisees tried to trap Jesus by presenting a woman who was caught in the act of adultery. They pointed to Moses' law, which prescribed stoning the woman to death.

The Pharisees believed they had Jesus in a trap. If he said to abide by Moses' law, he would reject the love, mercy, and forgiveness he preached. If he said to let her go, they could condemn him for ignoring the law.

But Jesus turned the table on the hypocrites. He bent over and wrote with his finger on the ground. When the Pharisees pressed him for an answer, Jesus called for the one who was without sin to cast the first stone.

As the accusers dropped their rocks and walked away, they were confronted with their own shortcomings.

As Jesus was left with the woman, he alone was qualified to judge. Instead, he used the opportunity to show mercy and to change a life.

What strikes me is that Jesus refused to judge—even though he was the only one present qualified to do so. In verses 15 and 16, he says, "You judge me by human standards, but I do not judge anyone. And if I did, my judgment would be correct in every respect because I am not alone. The Father who sent me is with me."

What was the result of Jesus refusing to judge the woman's sexual sin? She was most likely converted that day. Are we more likely to grow God's kingdom when we judge or when we show mercy, love, and forgiveness?

And yet, many who call themselves Christians take it upon themselves to judge others' sexual preferences and other activities.

From a faith perspective: Is this the way to expand the kingdom of God on earth?

From a political perspective: Do these conservatives, supposedly opponents of government intrusion in private lives, really want politicians intruding in their bedrooms?

Majority Rules

On Aug. 4, 2010, a federal judge ruled California's Proposition 8, which banned same-sex marriage, unconstitutional.

US District Judge Vaughn Walker ruled, "Proposition 8 does nothing more than enshrine in the California Constitution the notion that opposite-sex couples are superior to same-sex couples."[14]

In rejecting the statewide vote, Walker cited a 1943 Supreme Court decision that said, "Fundamental rights may not be submitted to a vote." He cited the due process and equal protection clauses.

Proposition 8 proponents argued that procreative capacity was a necessary prerequisite to obtaining a marriage license; that domestic partnerships are a (separate but equal?) substitute for marriage; that the state has a right to preserve traditional marriage through law; and that same-sex marriages would weaken families and the institution of marriage.

Walker rejected those arguments.

The ruling outraged same-sex marriage opponents (including the Faith and Freedom Coalition and many so-called evangelical Christians), who characterized the decision as "activist" and "a tyrannical assault on the Constitution." Several people I know claimed that the ruling (if not overturned on appeal) would lead to legalized polygamy, same-sex polygamy, and even marriage between humans and animals.

It seems to me there are two relevant aspects of marriage here: legal rights and religious rites.

---

[14]   US District Court for the Northern District of California, Perry [et al.] vs. Schwarzenegger [et al.], No. C 09-2292 VRW

Man's laws are designed, for the most part, to protect us from harming one another.

God's law is the moral imperative and designed to advance his kingdom "on earth as it is in heaven."

Legal Issues

Do I, as a heterosexual, have an inherent right to a legal status and privilege to which others, who are attracted to persons of the same gender, are not entitled? It seems obvious to me that I do not. How arbitrary is it to grant and withhold legal rights based on the gender to which one is attracted? It is as arbitrary as granting or withholding legal rights based on one's skin color. Thankfully, we no longer do that in America. While I do not claim to understand one man's attraction to another man or a woman's attraction to a woman, I cannot fathom why my preference gives me legal rights to which other Americans are not entitled—rights such as insurance benefits, tax deductions, and even hospital visiting privileges.

While Proposition 8 proponents argue that same-sex marriage harms traditional marriage, I fail to see how it threatens my relationship with my wife and soul mate.

As for the slippery-slope argument (that same-sex unions will lead to polygamy, homosexual polygamy, and even bestiality), that was not the question before the court. The question is: Should legal marriage rights be bestowed only on one man-one woman couples or should they also apply to two men or two women? Those who put forth this slippery-slope argument need only look at another example in our history to see its fallacy: Granting blacks the right to vote did not lead to suffrage for dogs and cats or horses. It simply eliminated a legal distinction based on the arbitrary trait of skin color. Similarly, the 1967 US Supreme Court decision in Loving v. Virginia, which legalized inter-racial marriage, has resulted in nothing more than black-white marriages that are in almost all respects identical to other marriages.

The procreation capacity argument is weak. If procreation capacity is a prerequisite to marriage, what do we do about sterile heterosexual men or women? Must they be prohibited from marriage? What about couples who choose not to have children (for whatever reason)?

Finally, can an "activist" judge simply reject the will of a majority of California voters?

As Walker stated in his ruling, "tradition alone . . . cannot form a rational basis for law."[15] One need only look to slavery for the answer here. A majority in favor and a tradition did not make the law any more valid. Our democracy was established specifically with checks, balances, and three branches to avoid the tyranny of the majority. The term "activist judge" is simply a rhetorical device invented by politicians to mean "a judge who disagrees with me."

As long as same-sex marriage creates no harm to others, the legal aspects of the debate seem to me to favor the Proposition 8 opponents.

Religious Rite

But what of the religious aspects of marriage?

The Old Testament clearly refers to homosexuality as an "abomination." God created Adam and Eve. Marriage is to be exclusively between one man and one woman. Of course, we also need to consider how the world was populated beyond Adam, Eve, Cain, and Abel (and after the flood); and consider many of David's sexual exploits. Somewhere in God's perfect plan, there had to be some sexually inappropriate activity taking place, even among his chosen.

The New Testament, however, teaches a new law based on love of others.

First John 4:7-11 (NLT): "Dear friends, let us continue to love one another, for love comes from God. Anyone who loves is a child of God and knows God. But anyone who does not love does not know God, for God is love. God showed how much he loved us by sending his one and only son into the world so that we might have eternal life through him. This is real love—not that we loved God, but that he loved us and sent his son as a sacrifice to take away our sins. Dear friends, since God loved us that much, we surely ought to love each other."

The New Testament teaches us not to judge others, however different they may be. It promotes justice and equality among people. My reading of the Bible does not lead me to think God condones discriminating against others on the basis of skin color, gender or other external, superficial characteristics over which they have no control—including sexual preference.

I'll let God judge homosexuals for their sin. I will not cast the first stone. I have enough sin of my own to worry about without concerning myself with others'.

---

[15]   Ibid.

Jesus used a parable of a Pharisee and tax collector to illustrate true righteousness. It seems especially appropriate in this case.

Luke 18:9-14 (NLT): "Then Jesus told this story to some who had great confidence in their own righteousness and scorned everyone else: 'Two men went to the Temple to pray. One was a Pharisee, and the other was a despised tax collector. The Pharisee stood by himself and prayed this prayer: "I thank you, God, that I am not a sinner like everyone else. For I don't cheat, I don't sin, and I don't commit adultery. I'm certainly not like that tax collector! I fast twice a week, and I give you a tenth of my income."

'But the tax collector stood at a distance and dared not even lift his eyes to heaven as he prayed. Instead, he beat his chest in sorrow, saying, "Oh God, be merciful to me, for I am a sinner."

'I tell you, this sinner, not the Pharisee, returned home justified before God. For those who exalt themselves will be humbled, and those who humble themselves will be exalted.'"

The Bible does not teach us to treat other people based on their similarity to ourselves—which, when we are honest, is really what a lot of this same-sex marriage debate boils down to. "If you are like me, you must be right in God's eyes. If you are not like me, God frowns on you."

Marriage is a gift from God. I know my life-love and soul mate is a gift from God. And God's gifts are intended for everyone. Nobody deserves God's grace, for example, but he gives it freely to all who would accept it. Why do we want to horde God's gifts for only ourselves and those we think are just like us—as the Pharisee does in the parable? Instead of defining ourselves based on our differences, God wants us to love and respect each other as brothers and sisters—all God's children in spite of our differences.

Paul wrote to the Romans, "Don't think you are better than you really are. Be honest in your evaluation of yourselves, measuring yourselves by the faith God has given us . . . . Don't just pretend to love others. Really love them . . . Live in harmony with each other. Don't be too proud to enjoy the company of ordinary people. And don't think you know it all." (Chapter 12, verses 3, 9, 16)

I don't pretend to understand homosexuality, but that doesn't mean I have to oppose it or judge it. What two loving people do in the privacy of their bedroom is no business of mine—or the government's. It is between them and God. It absolutely is not a reason to create a status of second-class citizen.

Judge Walker ruled wisely and correctly.

A question for same-sex marriage opponents—and perhaps this is where the conversation should start rather than end: Are you saying that homosexuals have no right to have a loving relationship? Or are you saying the relationship is okay, but you're drawing the line at a wedding?

Faith and Freedom Coalition: Wolves in Sheep's Clothing?

Ralph Reed is perhaps the most successful conservative American political activist of our generation. After interning at the College Republican National Committee in Washington, D.C., with Grover Norquist, under the leadership of Jack Abramoff, Reed was the first executive director of the Christian Coalition.

Under Reed's leadership, the Christian Coalition was instrumental in mobilizing Christian voters to support Republican candidates, especially in the 1990s. But Reed resigned his position in the middle of a federal investigation into the organization's finances.[16]

Later investigations,[17] including one that resulted in three felony convictions against Abramoff, revealed that Reed and the Christian Coalition received millions of dollars from Mississippi Native-American gambling interests in order to lobby against casino gambling and a lottery in Alabama. A US Senate Committee on Indian Affairs investigation concluded that Abramoff had Reed use Christian-based organizations (such as Focus on the Family and the Christian Coalition) to establish anti-gambling campaigns,

---

16   Federal Election Commission v. Christian Coalition, US District Court for the District of Columbia, civil action No. 96-1781 (JHG); http://lw.bna.com/lw/19990817/961781.htm

17   Final report before the committee on Indian Affairs, Oversight and Investigation; http://www.indian.senate.gov/public/_files/Report.pdf

resulting in the tribes paying Abramoff tens of millions of dollars to lobby on their behalf.

Today, Reed is the head of the Faith and Freedom Coalition, a non-profit that supports Republican causes. Republican candidates Newt Gingrich, Michele Bachmann, Herman Cain, John Huntsman, Ron Paul, Tim Pawlenty, Mitt Romney, and Rick Santorum all spoke at the FFC Conference in June 2011, as did Karl Rove, Donald Trump, and Haley Barbour, who was then governor of Mississippi.

Why do Ralph Reed and his cohorts purport to tell me the "Christian" position on various political issues? I consider myself a person of deep faith and I certainly believe that the United States is the greatest country in the world in large part because of the freedoms we embrace. But the FFC's so-called "scorecard," grading votes on various political and policy questions, does not represent the positions of all persons of faith. And, in my view, it does not represent the positions of many of us who call Jesus "Lord."

Most of the descriptions of the eleven votes targeted in the FFC scorecard are loaded with terms derived from the culture wars. They ignore or deliberately misrepresent legitimate details of the opposing view. If intentional, how is this not an outright violation of the Ninth Commandment? Nearly all of the programs and policies opposed by FFC are designed to improve the health and future prospects of Americans—especially those Jesus would call "the least of these" (Matt. 25:40).

The FFC website can be found at www.ffcoalition.org/.

The Faith and Freedom Coalition scorecard is in **bold font**, with my analysis in regular print:

1. Economic Stimulus. February 13, 2009. Roll call vote #70. President Obama's economic stimulus plan, $862 billion in new spending for pork-barrel projects, government jobs, and grants to states, paid for with deficit spending. Motion passed 246-183. A no vote is a vote for the FFC position.
Analysis: "Pork barrel projects" include improvements to bridges and roads and assistance to the domestic automobile industry (which saved hundreds of thousands of American jobs and was repaid by General Motors, with a slight profit going to the government coffers; i.e., taxpayers). "Government jobs" refers mostly to teachers, firefighters, and law enforcement officers. Grants to states were used for many purposes, including grants and loans to

finance higher education, job-training programs, and small businesses. The FFC description does not mention the total $260 billion in *tax reductions* given to working Americans. Isn't tax reduction supposed to be one of the FFC's primary objectives? The description also fails to mention the economic climate that forced the stimulus program in the first place: the worst recession since World War II. It also fails to mention that President Obama's Republican predecessor, George W. Bush, initially proposed the stimulus plan to avoid an economic depression and reduce the pain of the recession.

2. Hate Crimes. April 29, 2009. Roll call vote #223. Hate Crimes Prevention Act creates special classes of victims and would provide taxpayer funding for the prosecution of any crime either believed or thought to be motivated by sexual orientation or gender identity. Motion passed 249-175. A no vote is a vote for the FFC position.
Analysis: Reed and the FFC are saying that hate crimes against gays, lesbians, and bisexual or transgender individuals do not deserve the same rigorous prosecution as hate crimes against other individuals. The act merely adds protections for these individuals that are already afforded to other victim classes (based on race or gender, for example). In other words, we as a nation believe strongly in equal protection under the law, but the FFC believes some individuals are more equal than others are.

3. Out-of-control Spending. June 18, 2009. Roll call vote #408. Hiring Incentives to Restore Employment Act to increase government spending by over $69 billion while extending new government health care subsidies. Motion passed 259-157. A no vote is a vote for the FFC position.
Analysis: This law provided tax incentives (exemptions or credits) to nonprofit employers and small businesses that hired Americans who had been out of work for two months or more; increased tax credits for those businesses that retained such workers; and increased businesses' expensing allowance for depreciable assets. It also authorized public transportation spending. In spite of its heading on the scorecard "Out-of-control Spending," the law specifically complied with pay-as-you-go by increasing taxes on and reducing deductions for foreign banks that refuse to disclose American assets. The term "extending new government health care subsidies" refers to the effect the law has on COBRA (health insurance continuation for those

between jobs). In summary, it was a jobs bill that created tax breaks for small businesses.

4. Global Warming/Cap and Tax. June 26, 2009, Roll call vote #477. Creates a new government bureaucracy to regulate and limit carbon emissions, leading to billions in higher hidden taxes on the energy consumed by middle-class families. Motion passed 219-212. A no vote is a vote for the FFC position.

Analysis: Even those who deny climate change must believe we are to be good stewards of the Creation. Except, I suppose, when we have to pay to protect the planet. While cap and trade (referred to here as cap and tax) would result in higher energy costs, it is a free-market approach to attempt to reduce greenhouse gases. Rather than simply mandate reductions in carbon emissions, the act would create financial incentives for private industry to limit and reduce emissions.

5. Taxpayer-funding of Planned Parenthood. July 24, 2009. Roll call vote #643. Pence Amendment offered by Representative Mike Pence (R-IL) to the Health and Human Service appropriations bill to prohibit federal funds from going to Planned Parenthood. Motion failed 183-247. A yes vote was a vote for the FFC position.

Analysis: FFC is opposed to federal assistance to the only health-care provider many poor women will ever see. More than 90 percent of the services provided by Planned Parenthood are preventative, primary care, which helps prevent unintended pregnancies, reduces the spread of sexually transmitted diseases, and screens for early detection of cervical, breast and other cancers. Of course, the Hyde Amendment (in effect since 1976) already prohibits the use of federal funds to pay for abortions. So it must be other health-care services FFC wants to deny low-income women.

6. Taxpayer-funded Abortion. November 7, 2009. Roll call vote #886. Motion to Recommit Obamacare to apply Stupak-Pitts language to the Senate-passed version of Obamacare. Motion failed 187-247. A yes vote was a vote for the FFC position.

Analysis: As mentioned above, the Hyde Amendment has been in effect for more than thirty-five years. But this does not stop the FFC from using abortion as a political football. Even Bart Stupak, one of the bill's named sponsors, withdrew his opposition to the Patient Protection and Affordable

Care Act (referred to here as "Obamacare") when President Obama promised to sign an executive order confirming a ban on the use of federal funding for abortions. The president signed Executive Order 13535 on March 24, 2010, and as a result was criticized by both pro-life and pro-choice groups. Polls say a majority of Americans continues to oppose using federal tax dollars to fund abortions. Because of misinformation and an attempt to "divide" Americans for partisan political purposes, many do not know that federal law has prohibited such expenditures since 1976. If we are going to make public policy based on opinion polls, I would like to know how many Americans believe, as I do, that our tax dollars should not be used to kill innocent civilians in Iraq, Afghanistan, Pakistan, and elsewhere around the world.

7. Massive Tax Increase. December 9, 2009. Roll call vote #943. TARP 2, a $141 billion spending increase, which includes tax increases on small business owners. Motion passed 241-181. A no vote was a vote for the FFC position.

Analysis: TARP 2 required banks to undergo evaluation (stress test) to determine their solvency (the failure of big banks caused the global financial crisis that led to the current recession). It established a public-private investment fund to lend money to troubled banks to facilitate consumer and business lending, helping millions of consumers who were in danger of losing their homes due to the housing crisis. The FFC position is opposed to transparency and accountability for banks and opposed to helping Americans retain their homes.

8. Obamacare. March 21, 2010. Roll call vote #167. Barack Obama's government-run health-care plan, which will cost in excess of $1 trillion, cut Medicare $500 billion, and ration health care. Motion passed 220-211. A no vote was a vote for the FFC position.

Analysis: The Patient Protection and Affordable Care Act reforms the private health insurance market, provides better coverage for those with pre-existing conditions, and expands health-care coverage to include all individuals and families with incomes up to 133 percent of the poverty level. It establishes health insurance exchanges where consumers can comparatively shop for coverage in an open marketplace, establishes minimum standards for health insurance policies, removes annual and lifetime coverage caps, and provides tax credits to small businesses that make health insurance available to their employees. In addition, it improves Medicare prescription drug coverage and extends the life of the Medicare trust fund by at least twelve years. It makes health care available to forty million Americans who were without health insurance prior to its implementation. It does not provide taxpayer funding for abortions. It does not ration health-care services. It is not "government-run" health care. It allows patients to continue to make health decisions in consultation with the physician of their choice. And, according to the non-partisan Congressional Budget Office, it reduces the federal deficit by $143 billion over the first decade of its implementation and by $1.2 trillion in the second decade. In other words, "Obamacare" makes health insurance more available, more affordable, and more accountable while maintaining a privately run, free-market insurance industry. The Patient Protection and Affordable Care Act is probably the most intentionally misrepresented piece of legislation since the Civil Rights Act of 1964.

9. Gays in the Military. May 28, 2010. Roll call vote #336. Repealing the "don't ask, don't tell" policy. Motion passed 229-186. A no vote is a vote for the FFC position.
Analysis: Homosexuals are second-class citizens and don't have the right (or obligation) to help defend our country by serving in the military. Military leaders supported repealing the policy, which required tens of thousands of our brave men and women to live a lie in order to serve.

10. Restricting Freedom of Speech. June 24, 2010. Roll call vote #391. The DISCLOSE Act would have gutted the Supreme Court's Citizens United decision, restricting free speech rights for antitax and pro-family organizations while exempting labor unions. Motion to invoke cloture (end debate) failed 219-206. A no vote was a vote for the FFC position.
Analysis: The Democracy Is Strengthened by Casting Light On Spending in Elections Act would have prevented foreign influence in federal elections, prohibited government contractors from making expenditures with respect to federal elections, and established disclosure requirements to make federal election spending more transparent. Note that the FFC description says the bill would have exempted labor unions, but fails to mention exemptions carved out by lawmakers for other organizations, such as the National Rifle Association. It would have made American voters more informed about the decisions they make at the ballot box and about which special-interest

entities stand to lose or benefit from those decisions. It would not restrict free speech in any way, unless you believe the ability of unions, corporations, or lobbyists to make secret campaign contributions is the equivalent of free speech. Apparently, FFC believes democracy and freedom depend on a certain amount of voter ignorance at the ballot box.

11. Financial Regulation. June 30, 2010. Roll call vote #413. The Dodd-Frank bill created a new bureaucracy to regulate the financial industry and imposed new taxes and regulations, hurting community banks and small business. Motion passed 237-192. A no vote was a vote for the FFC position.

Analysis: The Restoring American Financial Stability Act of 2010 was a response to (and an attempt to avoid in the future) the financial shenanigans that led to the global financial crisis of the mid-to-late 2000s. Briefly, a few dozen investors, in collusion with major Wall Street banks and under the noses of the clueless credit-rating agencies, managed to transfer to their accounts (or else completely eliminate) trillions of dollars of publicly and privately held assets. For details of this debacle, read "The Big Short" by Michael Lewis.

What Makes Us Human?

The cover story of the March 2011 issue of The Atlantic magazine[18] was a fascinating excerpt from *The Most Human Human: What Talking with Computers Teaches Us about What it Means to Be Alive*, a book (Doubleday, March 2011) by Brian Christian about the Turing Test, a competition to discern machines from humans.

The competition consists of four judges typing questions to and soliciting responses from both human and digital (computer) participants. The judges do not know whether they are conversing with a human or a computer. After five minutes of textual interaction and ten minutes of reviewing the conversation, the judges must guess whether they were conversing with a human or with a computer.

The winner of the Loebner Prize is the computer programmer who can fool the most judges; the one who builds or programs the "Most Human Computer."

But Christian, who writes about philosophy and science, was interested in winning a secondary prize, the Most Human Human award, among the flesh-and-blood participants interacting with the judges.

As artificial intelligence programming has become more complex through the years, computers have been able to fool a larger percentage of judges. While scientists and philosophers from earlier eras tried to pinpoint

---

18   Brian Christian, "Mind vs. Machine," *The Atlantic*, March 2011, www.theatlantic. com/magazine/archive/2011/03/mind-vs-machine/8386/

what, exactly, sets the human race apart from other species, AI advances have changed the focus to what, if anything, sets us apart from computers.

To Christian, this raises a serious philosophical question: What, exactly, is it that makes us unique as a species?

And its corollary: Why, exactly, do we humans feel a need to be unique (or superior) to other animals—or superior to our digital counterparts?

"The story of the 21st century," Christian writes, "will be, in part, the story of the drawing and redrawing of these battle lines, the story of Homo sapiens trying to stake a claim on shifting ground, flanked by beast and machine, pinned between meat and math."

Christian makes some fascinating observations about past competitions involving man and machine.

For example, after chess grandmaster Gary Kasparov defeated IBM's Deep Blue in their first encounter in 1996, Kasparov and IBM agreed to a rematch the following year. When Deep Blue defeated Kasparov in 1997, Kasparov proposed another match for 1998. IBM declined and subsequently dismantled Deep Blue.

"The apparent implication," Christian writes, "is that—because technological evolution seems to occur so much faster than biological evolution (measured in years rather than millennia)—once the Homo sapiens species is overtaken, it won't be able to catch up. Simply put: the Turing Test, once passed, is passed forever. I don't buy it."

Christian concludes that the human race "got to where it is by being the most adaptive, flexible, innovative, and quick-learning species on the planet. We're not going to take defeat lying down."

Christian believes the first year computers fool a majority of the judges will "certainly be a historic one," but the following year's competition will be more telling. "[T]he one where we humans, knocked to the canvas, must pull ourselves up; the one where we learn how to be better friends, artists, teachers, parents, lovers; the one where we come back. More human than ever."

A telling example cited by Christian from a past Touring competition: The strategy of one past winner of the Most Human Human award was to be obnoxious—to use sarcasm and criticism in all his responses. It was effective in setting the participant apart from his artificial counterparts, but is that what sets us apart as humans?

The article is fascinating. It is even more so when viewed in context of the reactions from political extremes (right and left) to the rape of a female

CBS-TV news reporter in Liberation Square in Egypt while covering the toppling of the Mubarak regime in early 2011.[19]

Nir Rosen is a far-left journalist who calls for the elimination of Israel and who is a pro-Hamas Hezbollah apologist.

Debbie Schlussel is a far-right, racist anti-Muslim commentator.

Yet they both found delight in the public rape of reporter Lara Logan on February 11, 2011.

As Jeffrey Goldberg notes in his blog on *The Atlantic* Web site, "They come from radically different places on the political spectrum, and yet they share a common inhumanity."[20]

Does it really take a tragedy like this for extreme left and extreme right to agree? And, more disappointing: Must they agree on the side of inhumanity?

When we begin evaluating tragic or iconic events solely in terms of how they support our particular (partisan) political views, or when we use those events to support our positions rather than to evaluate them on a human level, we lose perspective on the relative importance of our ideology.

When partisans joke or make light of the rape of a CBS news reporter in the midst of a public square, our politics has become more important than that which makes us human.

Another example of this humanizing, inhuman behavior as it relates to politics:

On January 8, 2011, a gunman opened fire in a supermarket parking lot near Tucson, Arizona. Six people were killed, including a federal judge, and thirteen were wounded, including a US congresswoman, at a political "meet and greet" event at the supermarket. The alleged shooter, a twenty-two-year-old man who posted almost unintelligible rants online, was obviously mentally unstable. Courageous bystanders, some of them also victims, apprehended him. Various newspaper stories explored how the alleged perpetrator legally obtained a semi-automatic handgun and the permit to use it and revealed the medical conditions of the surviving victims at press time (old news in this era of the twenty-four hour news cycle on cable television). They rehashed the usual Second Amendment debates (more guns means more shooting deaths; more guns are in fact a deterrent to crime; and the

[19] Jeffrey Goldberg, "The Lunatic Left-Right Harmonic Rape Convergence Theory," *The Atlantic*, February 16, 2011, www.theatlantic.com/national/archive/2011/02/the-lunatic-left-right-harmonic-rape-convergence-theory/71350.
[20] Ibid.

inevitable NRA catchphrase "guns don't kill people . . . people kill people"). They revealed details of the lives of the various victims (including a dead nine-year-old girl who had enjoyed ballet and who, coincidentally, had been born on September 11, 2001).

But consuming the most column-inches, by far, were stories speculating whether incendiary rhetoric by far-right or far-left politicos did or did not prompt the shooting spree.

Pundits from across the political spectrum felt obligated to weigh in on the irresponsibility (or irrelevance) of a prominent politician's campaign material that urged supporters to "take out" certain incumbents in specific congressional districts. The campaign literature included a map with gunsight crosshairs focused on the relevant districts and a quote from the candidate encouraging like-minded Americans: "Don't retreat. Reload."

According to the news stories, the left-leaning pundits had been critical of the campaign material when it was unveiled ten months earlier. In the immediate aftermath of the tragedy, liberal pundits were saying, "we told you so," while conservative columnists pooh-poohed those notions and speculated that the current Democrat in the White House (a biracial Muslim born in Kenya who hates white people) was the shooter's motivation.

All this speculation occurred while investigators really had no idea yet about the gunman's motives.

Events like Lara Logan's rape and Gabrielle Giffords's shooting are horrifying and devastating. They are opportunities for us to show love and compassion and, hopefully, to open a dialogue and find common ground in our basic humanity.

When we use such tragic circumstances for political gain, however, we have indeed lost that which makes us human.

Constitutional Question: Make Me Pay for My Health Care or Make Me Pay for Someone Else's

Opponents of the individual mandate aspect of the Patient Protection and Affordable Care Act, passed by Congress and signed into law by President Barack Obama in March 2010, had better be careful what they wish for, because they just might get it.

If it is unconstitutional for the government to require Americans to purchase health-care coverage, then it is also unconstitutional to require health-care providers, such as hospital emergency rooms, to treat all patients who walk through their doors.

Do we really want to go down that road?

Opponents of Obamacare say Congress has no right to require Americans to purchase health-care coverage—or anything else, for that matter.

Sen. Orrin Hatch, R-Utah, called one federal court ruling striking down the individual mandate aspect of the PPACA "a victory for liberty." Once government can compel you to purchase insurance, Hatch said, it can tell you which car you have to buy.

It is a compelling argument—until one considers the ubiquitous and uniquely necessary nature of health care. Try, for a moment, to imagine any life lived without some contact with a medical provider. From the instant of birth to the moment of death, virtually all people rely on medical providers. It is literally a "life and death" matter.

US District Judge Henry E. Hudson said, in a forty-two-page opinion issued in December 2010, that the so-called individual mandate provision, which requires all Americans to buy some form of health insurance, would "invite unbridled exercise of the federal police powers."

"At its core," the judge ruled, "this dispute is not simply about regulating the business of insurance or crafting a scheme of universal health insurance coverage, its [sic] about an individual's right to choose to participate."

If that is indeed the case, then this is the very narrowest of decisions. Because, I would argue, almost everyone participates in health care at some point in his or her life. To say one has a right to choose not to participate in health care is absurd. Most of us have our first experience prior to or at birth and our last on our deathbed. There are usually thousands of events between. But there are admittedly a miniscule few people who, for religious reasons, refuse to *ever* receive medical treatment. (The law carves out an exemption for those people.)

Mandatory auto insurance is the oft-cited argument in response to opponents' objection to the individual health insurance mandate. Of course, one must not purchase auto insurance if one chooses not to drive. So we can create an exemption for anyone who agrees to never seek health care. Any takers?

The sole option for those who choose not to purchase insurance is to pay for their health care out of pocket—to self-insure. Unfortunately, such an option necessarily results in one of two negative impacts that I would argue overwhelmingly override the rights of those who would "prefer" not to buy health insurance.

Either you make hospitals require payment up front, before services are provided, or you make me pay for other peoples' health care.

Do we really want to make emergency rooms require payment before rendering services? How many thousands of lives will that cost each year? We prohibit emergency rooms from turning away patients precisely because medical care is vital; in fact, necessary. In many cases, scant seconds mean the difference between life and death. We Americans consider life to be so precious (it is an unalienable right endowed by our Creator) as to waive payment until after the threat has passed. Are those who object to the individual mandate's "destruction" of their "liberty" willing to abandon this principle? If not, then consider this question.

Which is worse: forcing me to pay for my health care or forcing me to pay for mine *and* someone else's?

Lawyers for the US government made precisely this case.

"The uninsured shift $43 billion in the cost of their care annually to other market participants," argued lawyers for Kathleen Sebelius, secretary of the Department of Health and Human Services, "including providers, patients (in the form of higher costs), insurers, and the insured population (in the form of higher premiums)."

Opponents of the individual mandate ignore not only the necessary and ubiquitous nature of medical care, but also the somewhat unique nature of insurance per se. Insurance is an unapologetically socialistic product in that it collects premiums from all participants and uses those proceeds to pay for costs all participants incur. It is based on "spreading the risk." The larger the pool of participants, the better is the deal for everyone. It is ideally a win-win-win situation for participants, providers, and the insurance company itself, which makes a tidy profit from the "leftovers."

That win-win-win breaks down, however, when participants and providers are forced to pay for costs incurred by patients who do not participate in the pool and are unable (or unwilling) to pay for services. The result is runaway health-care inflation.

It is somewhat ironic (and philosophically inconsistent) that, generally, those who oppose the individual mandate are the same folks who complain about having to subsidize medical care for the poor who cannot afford it. (They are also the same people, I suspect, who have already chosen to purchase health insurance.) The individual mandate offers a solution to that exact problem. And instead of using the emergency room to treat a child's sniffles (because they have neither money nor insurance), the poorer among us can visit the appropriate medical provider.

Either you can make me pay for my own health care or you can make me pay for mine and someone else's.

The converse situation, that the uninsured who actually pay their medical bills subsidize care for the insured, is also true. Medical providers bill uninsured patients at rates much higher—as much as 305 percent higher in urban hospitals, for example—than rates billed to insured patients.

Clearly, the system is broken. And health care inflation is out of control.

The historic health-care legislation, expanding coverage to thirty-two million Americans, is not a government-run program, as many opponents characterize it, but rather a program that will continue to allow patients to make medical decisions in consultation with their doctors, with private insurance companies administering payments. The legislation establishes regulations regarding what those insurance companies must provide, including a ban on lifetime limits on coverage (preventing insurers from withholding benefits for those with expensive treatments, such as cancer, for example), a restriction on annual limits, and a ban on dropping coverage when it is most needed (when the insured is sick, for example). It allows children to remain covered under parents' policies until their twenty-sixth birthday unless they obtain insurance elsewhere, and it prohibits discrimination against children with pre-existing conditions.

It also authorizes a new *competitive, private* health-care marketplace, or exchange, to be established in 2014, where Americans may purchase the coverage they feel is right for their circumstances.

In other words, it is a private sector, free-market solution. Ironically, when arguing before the US Supreme Court in 2012, opponents of the health-care law, so-called conservatives, said the government would have been within its constitutional power to impose a tax and institute government-run health care for all.

Michael A. Carvin, an attorney representing opponents, argued before the Supreme Court in March 2012 that, as an alternative to the individual mandate and the time-honored tradition in this country of providing care in emergency rooms regardless of ability to pay, the government could require patients to purchase health insurance at the point of service. This, Carvin said, would be within reason because it would require Americans to buy only after they had entered into the health-care market.[21]

As Justice Ruth Bader Ginsburg observed, however, there would be no incentive to purchase insurance early if patients knew they "had to be protected if they get insurance late." As a result, the whole insurance system fails.

An appropriate analogy would be fire protection. While many municipalities pay for fire departments through property taxes, local income taxes, or other mandatory assessments that allow the "insured" to share the

---

[21]   Oral argument transcript, US Supreme Court, 11-398 *DHHS v. Florida*, March 27, 2012, beginning at page 98.

cost responsibility, there are areas of rural America where fire districts offer optional protection. One example is in Obion County, Tenn., where a family lost all its possessions in a September 29, 2010 fire.

Gene Cranick, who lived outside the city, declined to pay an optional annual seventy-five dollar fee to the South Fulton fire protection district. His neighbors paid the fees for service on their own properties.

When his home was burning, Mr. Cranick pleaded on the telephone for the dispatcher to send firefighters. He said he'd pay the fee.

Firefighters responded, but did not try to extinguish the Cranick fire. They kept the fire from spreading, protecting the neighbors' homes.

Mr. Cranick was outraged. How could firefighters stand by and watch his house burn?

While it was unfortunate (and we can debate the moral obligation versus moral hazard dilemma firefighters faced once they responded), Mr. Cranick refused to accept responsibility for his personal choice not to pay for fire protection when he had the opportunity. He complained to the national media and received a lot of sympathetic coverage.

But what if everyone was allowed to pay the fee only at the point-of-service? Imagine trying to pay a fire insurance premium *after* the fire ignited. As Justice Ginsburg observed, there would be no incentive to purchase protection in advance. That means there would be no homeowners' fire insurance coverage at all (in the case of paying a premium at point-of-service) or no fire department at all (in a case similar to Cranick's).

The problem in this case is the existence of an option not to pay for fire protection. Call it "a la carte" government service.

Government is necessary because some things, by their very natures, are best done through the cooperation of all members of society. When we all share the cost of building roads or protecting citizens from crime or fire (or providing medical care), it is more equitable and practical. But the system collapses when some expect to receive services without paying their fair share of the cost.

This exemplifies where "pure" libertarianism fails.

Nonetheless, conservatives are determined to overturn "Obamacare." They misrepresent it as "government-run" health care that will "ration" care.

In fact, insurance companies already ration care. "Obamacare" expands coverage to tens of millions via a free-market approach utilizing private insurance companies.

The socialist alternative, of course, is single-payer, government-run health care, something similar to Medicare for all Americans.

Ironically, that is exactly what conservative PPACA opponents advocated as a preferred alternative when arguing before the US Supreme Court in March 2012.

Ground Zero Mosque and Religious Bias

Which country are we living in, anyway?

One might assume that private property ownership is among the most sacred rights championed by so-called conservatives. One would be wrong.

The controversy surrounding a proposed Islamic cultural center in lower Manhattan indicates, at least for the leaders of the Republican Party, that racial (cultural, religious) bias trumps constitutional private property rights.

Never mind that the Cordoba Initiative and the American Society for Muslim Advancement have owned property at 45-47 Park Place in downtown Manhattan for decades. Never mind that the group, headed by Imam Feisal Abdul Rauf, has every legal right to build a $100 million cultural center on its own property.

Rauf has written books on Islam and its place in Western society. He has publicly condemned the September 11, 2001, terrorist attacks on the United States and said terror has no place in Islam. His purpose for building the Islamic center, he told *The New York Times*, is to "send the opposite statement to what happened on 9/11."[22]

---

[22] "Muslim prayers and renewal near Ground Zero," *New York Times*, Dec. 8, 2009

Yet, Sarah Palin and Newt Gingrich oppose the Cordoba project. Palin urged "peaceful Muslims" to "refudiate" [*sic*] the project and called the proposal an "unnecessary provocation."

Since when is it provocative to exercise your constitutional private-property rights?

Gingrich argued that there should be no mosque near Ground Zero as long as there are no churches or synagogues in Saudi Arabia.

Since when do we base our American rights on the practices of Middle Eastern countries?

Palin and Gingrich ignore Americans' property rights in this case because their political aspirations depend on achieving the same goal as Osama bin Laden: driving a wedge between the West and Islam—even the peaceful form of Islam this project would promote. Palin and Gingrich need to oppose any project that will encourage peace between the cultures of the West and Middle East because they must have a boogieman to inspire fear among their political followers. Political expediency trumps the best interest of the people and peace between religions. Apparently, the strategy is effective. Millions of conservative Americans listen to Palin, Gingrich, and conservative commentators Rush Limbaugh and Glenn Beck and believe the misinformation.

Taking this anti-Muslim strategy to the extreme is the Florida Family Association, which describes itself as an organization promoting Christian, biblical values.

The FFA opposed a proposed television show on The Learning Channel, "All American Muslim," because, in the FFA's words, it depicted five Muslim families in Dearborn, Mich., "that appear to be ordinary folks." In other words, the FFA urged a boycott of TLC advertisers precisely because the show depicted ordinary, patriotic Muslim Americans.

Tim King, communications director for Sojourners, addressed the FFA's misguided position in a blog.[23]

King notes that, like many Americans, witnessing the terror attacks of September 11, 2001, was his first significant encounter with Islam, and that he did not have a "substantive" encounter with a Muslim for another five years.

---

[23] Tim King, "All-American Muslim: These People Are Dangerous," *Sojourners*, Dec. 13, 2011, www.sojo.net/blogs/2011/12/13/all-american-muslim-these-people-are-dangerous)

"While I was never actively prejudiced against any Muslims, I have to admit that my view of Islam in general was always refracted through the lens of 9/11. It was through personal encounters that let me see into another's life that my view of the world grew more accurate," King wrote. "Yes, there are those who call themselves Muslim that are violent and oppressive people and there are Muslims who are peaceful and loving.

"Yes, there are those who call themselves Christian that are violent and oppressive people and there are Christians who are peaceful and loving.

"My view of the world, and of Islam, got clearer as I got to know Muslims. Proximity allowed me to overcome a prejudice."

King wrote that "All American Muslim" was a means to expose and educate Americans "who might not otherwise have contact with 'ordinary' Muslims." It could also be a tool *against* extremism in some Muslim communities.

Like American racial bias before it, the attitude of Palin, Gingrich, and others who are "afraid" of Islam is based on a few heinous acts by a handful of extremists, ignorance, and a lack of exposure to ideals they instinctively oppose. The proposed mosque and information center in downtown Manhattan would expose Americans to peaceful Islam and a desire to live cooperatively. It would improve interfaith relations.

Just as Osama bin Laden before them could not, the Republican Party cannot afford such a cultural advance.

Even if that means the Republican Party must ignore one of conservatives' most sacred beliefs, private property rights.

Should We Celebrate? Retribution vs. Grace

In the wake of the announced capture and death of Osama bin Laden on May 1, 2011, by US military forces, there were impromptu celebrations in front of the White House, at Ground Zero in New York City, and at other places throughout the country.

In light of a number of seemingly contradictory Bible verses both warning against celebrating the death of any man—even an evil one—and proclaiming joy at the triumph of good over evil, were these celebrations appropriate among Christians?

I am not proud to admit my joy immediately after President Barack Obama announced the death of bin Laden. I felt a tinge of guilt as I watched people dance for joy in the streets.

After a couple of days of soul-searching and self-examination, I have decided that both reactions are appropriate. Your results may vary.

While it is not appropriate, in my opinion, to celebrate the death of another of God's children, it is appropriate to bask in the triumph of good over evil, at the end to an age of uncertainty and terror, and at the delivery of justice.

Osama bin Laden was responsible for the deaths of thousands of innocent people in terror attacks around the world. Most of us will always remember the sickness we felt on September 11, 2001, as two passenger planes crashed into the World Trade Center tower in New York City and another targeted the Pentagon in our nation's capital. In addition to the thousands of people killed on that day, bin Laden in effect punched each and every American in the gut and then gloated. So some sort of relief is only natural.

What is in my mind completely inappropriate is the politicization of the event in its aftermath. Partisans seized on the opportunity to promote political agendas from torture justification to insistence that post-mortem photographs of bin Laden be publicly displayed.

Our focus should be on the future, on how this historic event can shape our policies and what we can learn from it.

OBL distorted the religion of Islam. His particular flavor of hate turned perfectly innocent people against one another based on false teachings and a perversion of faith. He managed to justify and motivate Muslim violence against Christians and Jews and even against other Muslims.

As a result of bin Laden's unconscionable acts, many misguided Americans misunderstand the Islamic faith and hate all Muslims—to the point where we tolerate the torture of other human beings and object to the building of mosques and Islamic centers designed to bridge the gap between people of differing faiths.

What can we learn from bin Laden's death and achieve by moving forward?

We can reunite with our brothers and sisters of different faiths. We can seek an end to failed wars that are based on false premises and result in the deaths of millions of innocents. We can reject the Machiavellian rationalization that terror justifies torture. We can find more appropriate and effective ways to settle our differences.

We can promote love and peace.

We can display grace rather than continue seeking revenge.

We celebrate the death of Osama bin Laden not out of a sense of retribution, but because justice has been served and the world can be a better place as a result.

In refusing to release the photographs of the slain bin Laden, President Obama took the high ground. It was a first, hopeful indication that we have turned the corner and are headed in a more graceful direction.

Unions and the
Demonizing Wedge

Maryemily and I were listening to a Christian radio station the other day (to my Church of Christ friends who are now worried about my soul: We sometimes like to listen to praise and worship music as an alternative to songs about drinkin' and cheatin') when an interview came on that shocked me.

The person being interviewed was Finn Laursen, executive director of Christian Educators Association International. The interviewer asked him this loaded question: "Is the National Education Association really as evil as we hear it is?"

"In a word," Laursen responded, "Yes."

To substantiate his claim, Laursen pointed out that, at that year's NEA meeting in New Orleans, the largest professional organization and labor union in the United States recognized a new caucus: the NEA Drag Queen Caucus.

"I think that just speaks for itself," Laursen said. End of radio segment.

Maryemily and I looked at each other in disbelief.

"That just doesn't sound right," she said. I agreed, thinking that, even if such a caucus did exist, it would probably be called something different.

I also had questions I was dying to ask Mr. Laursen.

1) On a secular level, are you saying that these dues-paying members of the NEA have no right to caucus to ensure their voices are heard and their

interests represented and considered within the organization (but those whose beliefs conform to yours are, of course, entitled to representation)? And,

2) As a Christian leader, supposedly representing the interests of thousands or millions of Christians, are you assuming that God somehow loves these, his children, less than he loves you? Because you are without sin, right?

3) More to the point: How does your open and public disdain for these "others" exemplify your Christian love? Do you believe your words and actions are designed to bring them into the fold (if they are not already)? Or is it possible your words and actions could alienate them (and others) from the church?

When we got home, I did some research and found a Web site that purports to bring a Christian perspective to the news, OneNewsNow. It carried a more extensive portion of the Laursen interview.[24]

"They already have had the Gay, Lesbian, Bisexual, [and] Transgender Caucus and apparently felt that the drag queens needed their own caucus," explains Finn Laursen, executive director of Christian Educators Association International (CEAI).

The story included a link to the official NEA listing of the organization's caucuses: http://www.nea.org/assets/docs/nea-handbook-recognized-caucuses.pdf.

The link is no longer valid. But when it was, there was no "drag queen" caucus listed.

Which raises all kinds of other red flags in my mind.

Is Mr. Laursen making this up? Does he feel so invested in the culture wars that he, a professing Christian and leader, has to make up a boogieman to demonize an organization representing teachers all across the country? Is a Ninth Commandment violation an appropriate tactic for a Christ-follower?

Or, if there is, in fact, an unlisted "drag queen caucus," how is that caucus less deserving of proportional representation than a caucus of Christians? I would bet there are some NEA members who would qualify for membership in *both* caucuses.

"America, I think, needs to respond and to realize what the National Education Association stands for; they're not hiding it. It's appalling to many

---

[24]   Bill Bumpas, "NEA Celebrates 'Drag Queen' Teachers," OneNewsNow.com, July 15, 2010, www.onenewsnow.com/Education/Default.aspx?id=1088280

of our conservative Christian educators who, in their own lives, could not support this kind of thing but find that their dues are being used to support just those kinds of things," Laursen added at the end of the Web article.

While many Christian educators may not be able to support "this kind of thing" in their own lives, I pray they would support rather than demonize their fellow children of God and try to influence lives positively rather than driving wedges between them.

All Eyes on Wisconsin

More recently, in February 2011, Republican Wisconsin Gov. Scott Walker took a swipe at unionized public employees by proposing a bill eliminating collective bargaining rights over pensions and health care and limiting pay raises to the rate of inflation. The bill also required public-sector unions to recertify each year and ended the state's practice of automatic union dues collection.

The governor characterized his proposal as a protection for taxpayers, who pay teachers' salaries, pensions, and other benefits. (The bill exempted the state's police officers, troopers, and firefighters.)

Tens of thousands who protested in Madison in the following months characterized the bill as an attempt to eliminate public-employee unions.

There are many convincing arguments that unions have outgrown their function in the United States, but there is no doubt that unions were once necessary and built the middle class in America in the twentieth century. The power to bargain collectively protected workers from government and private industry abuses in terms of benefits and workplace safety rules.

Unfortunately, many unions eventually overstepped their powers and bargained their members (and employers) out of business. Some unions have gone too far in protecting disgruntled and unqualified workers. In addition, corruption and greed have irreparably tarnished the reputations of some unions.

In other words, neither side is treating the other in a manner they would like to be treated. Even though union members are dependent on their employers, and the employers are equally dependent on workers, the relationship has become adversarial instead of mutually beneficial.

Have unions outlived their purpose in the United States?

Probably not. But some reforms are needed.

Unfortunately, neither unions nor their opponents seem to be willing to make concessions that would benefit both.

Many companies and some units of government recognize the need to treat workers fairly and compensate them adequately. Still others, however, are willing to injure their workers in order to pad the bottom line. Sometimes finances and profit take priority in matters in which safety and fairness should be the primary consideration.

And, of course, there is the political aspect.

Unions traditionally donate money to Democratic causes and candidates (because that party traditionally supports the policies and values that protect its members). Businesses traditionally donate to Republicans using the same rationale. Is it any wonder there is so much animosity about the US Supreme Court decision in Citizens United v. Federal Election Commission, which held that corporations (and unions) are entitled to free-speech rights and that expenditures to political campaigns are a form of "speech"?

But let's get back to the Wisconsin controversy.

First, politicians on both sides of the aisle acted irresponsibly. Democrats, the minority party in the Wisconsin legislature, initially left the state and went into hiding in order to prevent a vote on the union-busting bill. They abdicated their responsibility as elected officials.

Republicans who supported the bill in effect acknowledged they had abdicated their responsibility to negotiate with unions. After all, collective bargaining is supposed to be just that: a negotiation between unions and their representatives on one side and, in the case of public employees, government representatives on the other. If public unions had become too powerful and rich in Wisconsin, it was with the concurrence of elected politicians who negotiated and ratified the contracts.

The controversy attracted national attention and cost two out-of-state politicians their jobs for their partisan participation.

Indiana Deputy Attorney General Jeffrey Cox was fired after he suggested that Gov. Walker should use live ammunition against protesters in the capitol.

Carlos Lam, a deputy prosecutor in Johnson County, Indiana, resigned after it was revealed that he had suggested that Walker fake an attack on himself by someone pretending to be sympathetic to the unions.[25]

---

[25]   Debra Cassens Weiss, "A second Indiana prosecutor is out of a job for unusual advice to Wisconsin governor," *ABA Journal*, March 25, 2011.

The prosecutors allowed a "win at all costs" attitude to blind them to humanity (in Cox's case) and truth (in Lam's). They let partisan politics trump qualities such as honor, integrity, and cooperation.

Sadly, that kind of unethical behavior is not unique to the Wisconsin controversy, and self-professed Christians are not immune to such temptations.

The Bible and
the Constitution

The Bible and the US Constitution are perhaps the two documents with the most varied interpretations.

Nearly everyone is certain his interpretation is correct and rejects others who read it differently.

Maybe this disparity is a result of the powerful impact those two documents have on our lives.

Harold Camping, president of Family Radio (www.familyradio.com), initially predicted the rapture (1 Thess 4:16-17) would occur May 21, 1988. When that didn't happen, he revised his calculation to September 7, 1994. After the world didn't end then, he projected a May 21, 2011 date, based on the Bible verse that says one thousand years is as a day to God, the date of Noah's flood (the fourteenth day of second month in 4990 BC, which somehow to Camping translated to May 21), and adding seven "God" days (or millennia). Camping's math is based on Daniel 12:9-13 and Revelation 22:10.

Camping was "absolutely certain" May 21, 2011, was the Day of Judgment. When May 21 passed, Camping recalculated and was certain October 21, 2011, was the day of the Rapture.

Yet (assuming you are reading this), here we are.

This is not to ridicule Camping (although I personally believe his endeavor to be folly, see Matthew 24:36), but to show that even those who are absolutely certain of immensely important things can be absolutely, immensely wrong.

So who is to say I am not wrong? Or you?

The same goes for the Constitution.

Strict Construction vs. Living Document

Many of the strict interpretationists (or originalists) insist that any deviation from the original intent of the Constitution weakens it. This approach can be helpful, but becomes absurd when taken to its extreme.

For example, many—especially in the South—insist that the Fourteenth Amendment's citizenship clause, which overruled Dred Scott v. Sandford, applies only to those who were slaves at the time the amendment was adopted (July 9, 1868). Thus, they argue, children born in the United States to parents who are citizens of another country should not be granted US citizenship. (The Supreme Court ruled otherwise.) After Barack Obama made public his long-form birth certificate, which showed he was born in Hawaii, so-called "birthers" turned to this interpretation of the Fourteenth Amendment to continue to assert he is not constitutionally qualified to be president.

It is an example of the tail wagging the dog; interpreting the document in a way that supports one's partisan political views, when in fact one's positions should be framed by the document and its underlying principles.

What is truly telling is that, at other times, strict interpretationists seem to ignore the plain language of the Constitution. Take the Second Amendment, for example: "A well regulated Militia, being necessary to the security of a free State, the right of the people to keep and bear Arms, shall not be infringed."

Most strict interpretationists, who tend to be gun-rights advocates, simply ignore the word "regulated." They assert the government has no power at all to regulate "arms." This, of course, leads to the absurd conclusion that every American has the right to "keep and bear" a thermonuclear warhead. The amendment, after all, refers to "arms."

Let's consider another way to approach the interpretation problem: What if the framers of the Constitution expected future generations to consider the document with common sense and in the context of current circumstances?

Must we ignore air-traffic control or throw out all traffic laws just because the Constitution is silent about airplanes and automobiles? Or should we apply the principles of the Constitution to the use and regulations of airplanes and automobiles?

Many conservatives today refer to judges who consider the Constitution a "living" document as "activist" judges. But judicial activism is actually interpreting the Constitution (and other laws) in a manner that fits one's own partisan political view. And judges on both extremes are equally guilty.

Westboro Baptist Church: A Case to Study

There are thousands of court cases where interpretations of the Bible and the Constitution converge and sometimes clash. Perhaps none is as divisive as the recent 8-1 US Supreme Court decision in favor of Westboro Baptist Church and its right to protest at military funerals.

Westboro is certainly not a mainstream Christian movement. Its membership is about forty, nearly all of whom are members of Pastor Fred Phelps's family. But its primary belief is firmly based in a literal interpretation of the Bible.

Westboro believes God hates homosexuals and condemns the US military, including all its members regardless of sexual orientation, because the armed services tolerate homosexuals. The church's Website is http://www.godhatesfags.com. Sister sites promoted there include GodHatesIslam.com, GodHatesTheMedia.com, GodHatesTheWorld.com, JewsKilledJesus.com, PriestsRapeBoys.com, and BeastObama.com.

Members of the church infamously travel to military funerals and cruelly protest—loudly—in order to disrupt what should be solemn and respectful occasions honoring those brave soldiers and sailors who gave their lives defending our country. They carry signs saying things like "God hates America," "Thank God for 9/11," "Pray for more dead soldiers," "You're going to hell," and "Thank God for dead soldiers."

After the group protested at the funeral of fallen Marine Matthew Snyder in Maryland in March 2006, Snyder's father, Albert, sued the church and won a multimillion-dollar judgment. The case was appealed all the way to the US Supreme Court.

But in March 2011, the court ruled 8-1 that Westboro's hateful public speech is protected by the Constitution's First Amendment. Chief Justice John Roberts's opinion concluded that Westboro's signs and speech "highlighted issues of public import," and were thus immune from liability.

Westboro may have chosen the picket location to increase publicity for its views, and its speech may have been particularly hurtful to Snyder. That does not mean that its speech should be afforded less than full First Amendment protection under the circumstances of this case, Roberts ruled.[26]

The court's most conservative and liberal members concurred with Roberts's opinion. Only conservative Justice Samuel Alito dissented.

How ironic (and sad) that the victim of the hateful and hurtful actions and words of WBC members was the grieving family of a young man who gave his life defending the right of WBC members to spew their particular flavor of hate and intolerance.

This, apparently (like tolerating pornography and obscenity), is the price we pay to protect freedom.

---

[26]   Paraphrased, No. 09-751 *Snyder v. Phelps [et al]*, p. 9-10.

Romney:
The Sky Is Falling

I n announcing his candidacy for the Republican presidential nomination on June 2, 2011, Mitt Romney rewrote history. He said that the US economy has grown worse during Barack Obama's presidency. To be exact, he said:

> "Barack Obama has failed America.
> When he took office, the economy
> was in recession. He made it worse.
> And he made it last longer."

Fact check:

The stock market: In January 2009, when Obama took office, the Dow Jones Industrial Average was 8,077. Due to inertia, it continued to fall to a low of about 6,500 in March of that year. As of January 20, 2012, the Dow was about 12,500. In May 2012, the Dow was above 13,000.

In January 2001, when George W. Bush took office, the Dow was at 10,000. As noted above, it was about 2,000 points *lower* when Bush left office eight years later.

So the Dow lost a net of 2,000 points during Bush's eight years (actually 8,000 from its high of 16,000), but gained 5,000 during Obama's first three years.

Jobs: In January 2009, the unemployment rate was 7.8 percent (per US Department of Labor Bureau of Labor Statistics). In May 2012, the unemployment rate was at 8.1 percent and declining.

In January 2001, unemployment was 4.2 percent. So unemployment nearly doubled during the Bush years and has been falling (slowly but steadily) since October 2009. In terms of actual jobs, the economy shed 185,000; 233,000; 178,000; 231,000; 267,000; 434,000; 509,000; 802,000; 619,000; and 820,000 jobs during the final ten months of the Bush presidency, for a total of 4,278,000 nonfarm jobs lost.

Through April 2012, the economy under Obama had posted job gains in twenty-six consecutive months.

Realizing that the economy does not turn around overnight, how can Romney say with a straight face that the economy has grown worse during President Obama's administration? The Dow has nearly doubled. The unemployment rate is falling. Companies are hiring workers at a faster clip than layoffs.

Isn't Romney supposed to be the "smart" GOP candidate? He is former CEO at Bain Capital. The centerpiece of his presidential campaign is the assertion that he is the one "who understands how the economy works." He understands the market and jobs. But he misrepresents the truth, at least in terms of the Obama administration's record.

Does he think if he continues to say it, people will take it as truth? Apparently. Other Republicans have adopted the same talking points. When weekly, monthly, and quarterly employment numbers are released, Fox News commentators invariably refer to them as "dismal" or "disappointing," even though the trend is toward more jobs and less joblessness.

Newt Gingrich's presidential candidacy briefly surged when he adopted the catchphrase "the food stamp president" to describe Obama. Gingrich asserted that the president and his administration have a political motivation to keep the poor dependent on government assistance.

The fact that so many Americans require government assistance is absolutely a reason for despair. It does not necessarily follow that the president is to blame or that he wants Americans to remain poor. But ascribing false motives has become a favorite strategy for politicians in both parties.

For the record: In March 2012, forty-six million Americans (in twenty-two million households) were participating in the Supplemental Nutritional

Assistance Program.[27] About half of them were younger than eighteen, and 8 percent were older than sixty. Forty-one percent of participants lived in households where someone is employed.

More broadly, a report,[28] based on budget and census data, was released in February 2012 by the Center on Budget and Policy Priorities. The report shows that 91 percent of the benefit dollars that entitlement and other mandatory programs spend goes to assist people who are elderly, seriously disabled, or members of working households "not to able-bodied, working-age Americans who choose not to work."

Further, seven of the remaining 9 percent, the report notes, goes for medical care, unemployment insurance benefits (qualification for which requires a work history), social security survivor benefits for children of deceased workers, and social security benefits for retirees aged sixty-two to sixty-four.

That leaves two percent of the benefits for the so-called "lazy poor."

Certainly, Romney and Gingrich have genuine differences in philosophy from President Obama. Why not focus on those differences instead of just making things up or misrepresenting the truth?

---

[27]   "Policy basics: Introduction to the Supplemental Nutrition Assistance Program," Center on Budget and Policy Priorities, April 18, 2012; http://www.cbpp.org/cms/index.cfm?fa=view&id=2226

[28]   "Contrary to "Entitlement Society" Rhetoric, Over Nine-Tenths of Entitlement Benefits Go to Elderly, Disabled, or Working Households," Center on Budget and Policy Priorities, Feb. 10, 2012; http://www.cbpp.org/cms/index.cfm?fa=view&id=3677

The Problem with Fox News (and MSNBC)

A story about vote fraud in the 2010 US Senate election in Minnesota exemplifies why I enjoy watching Fox News for entertainment, but fear what it does to society.[29]

The story takes on faith the assumption made by Minnesota Majority, the conservative group who conducted an investigation into a US Senate vote recount, that every one of the 341 convicted felons it discovered had voted illegally, voted for the Democratic candidate Al Franken. That is the only way Fox News can conclude that the election—decided by 312 votes in a recount—was "stolen by the lib," as one of my good friends (a loyal Fox News viewer) concluded.

To be clear: I think voter fraud is potentially one of the biggest threats to our society because it dilutes and distorts the democratic process on which our elected government is established. It is important that election officials follow up on the investigation's findings and act to ensure this kind of fraud can't be repeated.

But the conclusion by Minnesota Majority, repeated by Fox News and conveyed to its audience, is that Franken won the election *because of* this voter fraud. To come to that conclusion is ludicrous. One could just as easily

---

[29]   Ed Barnes, "Felons Voting Illegally May Have Put Franken Over the Top in Minnesota, Study Finds", *Fox News*, July 12, 2010, www.foxnews.com/politics/2010/07/12/felons-voting-illegally-franken-minnesota-study-finds/

assert that Franken would have won the election by 653 votes (assuming all fraudulent voters cast ballots for the Republican candidate, incumbent Norm Coleman, which would be just as ludicrous).

In our democratic system, we vote anonymously. We have secret ballots. There is no way to track for whom these 341 ineligible voters cast their ballots.

But this is the evil genius of Fox News.

Any "real" journalist knows you can't jump to the conclusion, without evidence, that every one of those convicted felons who voted illegally cast his ballot for Franken. It is highly likely that at least some of them voted for Coleman. There is no possible way for us to know how the fraudulent voters cast their ballots. But isn't it possible—perhaps likely—that the illegal votes went to Franken and Coleman in roughly the same ratio as the rest of the votes overall, roughly 171-170, in an election where more than 2.88 million votes were cast?

But Fox News (and more generally its parent company, News Corporation) isn't interested in straight journalism. It is advocacy journalism.

Again, don't misconstrue what I am saying. I have no problem with advocacy journalism as long as it represents itself as such. But Fox News promotes itself as "Fair and Balanced" and says "We report, you decide." Yet, every single day, the network presents stories that shed the least flattering light on Democrats. Sometimes it omits facts. It takes quotes or actions out of context daily. Favorite strategies include *ad hominem* attacks, hasty generalizations, and guilt by association (even when there is no association). Many Fox pundits who profess to be Christians do not hesitate to violate the Ninth Commandment.

The network is not interested in philosophic consistency, either. Every day you can hear experts extolling the free market, claiming that private enterprise is always superior to government participation. But Fox has never acknowledged such conservative Obama initiatives as privatization of space exploration, reduction in government employment while private employment slowly rises, establishment of "pay-as-you-go" in Congress, the success of resuscitating the failing banking and domestic auto industries, a dramatic reduction in illegal immigration, extension of the Bush income tax cuts, or establishing a bipartisan commission to make recommendations to reduce the federal debt. Fox would praise all of those conservative accomplishments if the president were a Republican.

Fox News' evil genius is that it preys on an assumption prevalent among the conservative movement that can be summed up generally by "You are not like me. (Thus you must be the opposition.)"

In the case of the Minnesota election, the assumption is that, since the vote fraud was perpetrated by convicted felons, they must have all voted for the Democrat (liberal, "other") Al Franken. If they are convicted felons, after all, they aren't like me. They *must have* voted for the Democrat.

I have done the math. The election was decided by a difference of 312 votes. There were 341 fraudulent ballots allegedly cast. For the illegal voters to have "put Franken over the top," as the Fox headline asserts, at least 327 of the 341 fraudulent voters (or nearly 96 percent) must have cast ballots for Franken (leaving less than 5 percent of the fraudulent voters to opt for Coleman in an election that was split 50 percent to 50 percent).

Fox News must know the assumption that *all* illegal voters cast ballots for Al Franken is a false premise leading to a logical fallacy. But as an advocacy group, Fox News passes the conclusion on to its audience anyway. And many—likely most Fox viewers—take that conclusion on faith without thinking for themselves or asking if something is wrong with the logic. In fact, Fox often trumpets its distinction from "mainstream" media. And many viewers take the bait, rationalizing that they're getting the news "from a conservative perspective."

A more recent, and perhaps more blatant, example at Fox is the opinion piece by Peter J. Johnson Jr. broadcast Friday, Jan. 6, 2012.[30]

Johnson showed clips from 2008 of then-candidate Barack Obama denouncing then-President George W. Bush's practice of adding clarifying or modifying statements when he signed legislation into law. Obama clearly said he thought the practice was an inappropriate abuse of executive power as a way to conduct a constitutional "end around" Congress.

But, as Johnson points out, Obama used a signing statement on December 31, 2011. Righteous indignation follows. If Obama believes signing statements are an abuse of power, he has an obligation to either sign the bill or veto it, Johnson says.

The problem: Johnson never says exactly which legislation Obama clarified with a signing statement. In the piece, Johnson goes on to talk about Obama making administrative appointments during a Congressional

---

[30]   Peter Johnson, "President Obama Embraces Signing Statements?", *Fox News*, Jan. 6, 2012, http://video.foxnews.com/v/1369313203001

recess (an issue completely unrelated to the clips or signing statement) leading viewers to believe that was the nature of Obama's own "end run" around Congress.

But the signing statement in question was, in fact, about the 2012 National Defense Authorization Act. Among other provisions, the bill authorized the administration to detain terror suspects—including American citizens—indefinitely and without trial.

Obama's actual statement (not shown or discussed on Fox) said he signed the bill "chiefly because it authorizes funding for the defense of the United States . . . crucial services for service members and their families and vital national security programs that must be renewed."[31]

Obama believes, however, that the indefinite detention of American citizens violates the Fifth (and Fourteenth) Amendment right of due process.

"My administration will not authorize the indefinite military detention without trial of American citizens," Obama's signing statement said, in part. "Indeed, I believe that doing so would break with our most important traditions and values as a nation."[32]

Any responsible news organization would have told the entire story and informed its followers exactly what Obama said and about what issues were in play. It might have pointed out that members of Congress overwhelmingly supported the bill in spite of its unprecedented attack on Americans' rights.

But if Fox had done that, one suspects, most of its viewers would have agreed with Obama on this one. Many of my conservative friends have expressed disbelief that Congress would have endorsed a policy that so blatantly violates Americans' rights. The vast majority of them would have sided with Obama on this issue, no matter how much they dislike him.

Wikipedia defines advocacy journalism thus:

"Advocacy journalism is a genre of journalism that intentionally and transparently adopts a non-objective viewpoint, usually for some social or political purpose. Because it is intended to be factual, it is distinguished from propaganda. It is also distinct from instances of media bias and failures of objectivity in media outlets, which attempt to be—or which present themselves as—objective or neutral.

---

[31] "Statement by the president on H.R. 1540," White House press office, Dec. 31, 2011.

[32] Ibid.

"Traditionally, advocacy and criticism are restricted to editorial and op-ed pages, which are clearly distinguished in the publication and in the organization's internal structure. News reports are intended to be objective and unbiased. In contrast, advocacy journalists have an opinion about the story they are writing. For example, that political corruption should be punished, that more environmentally friendly practices should be adopted by consumers, or that a government policy will be harmful to business interests and should not be adopted. This may be evident in small ways, such as tone or facial expression, or in large ways, such as the selection of facts and opinions presented."[33]

Advocacy journalism has a long tradition, dating back to before our country was founded. It has an important place in shaping public opinion and introducing various and opposing views into the public discussion of ideas.

The problem arises when such advocates hide their biases and cloak their perspectives in a disguise of objectivity, leading readers and viewers to believe they are getting "news" when they are, in fact, consuming opinion and analysis intentionally composed to promote a political party or philosophy.

A look at the Fox lineup is revealing. "Journalists" in its lineup include former (or current) Republican politicians Mike Huckabee, Newt Gingrich, Sarah Palin, Oliver North, Rudy Giuliani, Dana Perino, and Karl Rove. According to The New Republic, Steven Milloy, a former commentator at Fox News, received $90,000 from ExxonMobil and nearly $100,000 a year from Philip Morris during the time he criticized the science behind global warming and secondhand smoke as a carcinogen.[34]

Also telling is a $1 million donation to the Republican Governors Association by Fox parent company News Corporation in June 2010.

As long as Fox News continues its advocacy journalism while portraying itself as a "real" news organization, I believe it is appropriate to refer to it as Faux News.

---

[33] Wikipedia contributors, "Advocacy journalism," Wikipedia, The Free Encyclopedia, http://en.wikipedia.org/w/index.php?title=Advocacy_journalism&oldid=484214498 (accessed June 11, 2012).

[34] Thacker, Paul D. (February 6, 2006). "Smoked Out: Pundit for Hire". The New Republic (The New Republic). http://www.tnr.com/article/104858/smoked-out (retrieved July 17, 2012)

Similarly, cable news channel MSNBC should replace its catchphrase "lean forward" with "lean left." Former primetime anchor Keith Olbermann is also a donor to left-leaning politicians.

The solution, of course, is for Americans to get their news from a variety of sources. Unfortunately, many Fox viewers distrust any other source that doesn't present the news through the prism of Republican politics.

The wild popularity of the network among conservatives has caused some Republicans to speculate that the network's activism is even stronger than the political party's policy positions. David Frum, former speechwriter for George W. Bush, said this about Fox on ABC's nightly news magazine "Nightline" on March 23, 2010: "Republicans originally thought that Fox worked for us and now we're discovering we work for Fox."

Torture and American Exceptionalism

America is the land of opportunity. It is exceptional for many reasons, including the American Dream of upward mobility, the principle of individual responsibility, and the ability to achieve economic prosperity based on hard work. America loves peace, nurtures liberty, respects human rights, and embraces the rule of law. It believes in equality and rejects class distinctions, imperialism, and war. America is virtuous. Its system of checks and balances is designed to prevent the centralization of power in any person or organization.

As President Abraham Lincoln said in his address on November 19, 1863, at Gettysburg, Pennsylvania, our country was "conceived in liberty and dedicated to the proposition that all men are created equal." It boasts a government "of the people, by the people, for the people."

America is exceptional because of its values. They are based on Judeo-Christian values—although Judaism and Christianity hold no monopoly on those standards. Many of the world's great faiths (including Buddhism, Confucianism, Hinduism, Islam, and Taoism), and even philosophies based on no faith, embrace the concept of human dignity and some articulation of the Golden Rule.

Yet it is not just Americans that believe our country is exceptional. Foreigners look to the United States as a beacon on a hill. Since its establishment more than 235 years ago, it has been a constant refuge for those fleeing corrupt or immoral regimes. There may be no prouder moment in our history than the middle of the twentieth century, when young American men and women gave their blood, sweat, tears, and lives in Europe and the Pacific to save the world from the oppression and domination of white supremacist Nazi Germany and imperialist Japan.

Certainly, our nation has had its growing pains and moral failings. Slavery and the treatment of Native Americans are blemishes in our past. It was only fifty years ago that our laws codified equal rights for African Americans.

But we have moved beyond these disgraces. Just as we emerged from the tests of the Civil War and World War II stronger because we pursued our values, we continue to grow and rectify the errors of the past. In November 2008, a majority of Americans went to the polls and elected an African American president—a collective act thought inconceivable just twenty years ago.

But a little more than a decade ago, a single heinous act by a group of radical foreign extremists changed America—and changed the world.

The September 11, 2001, terror attacks on innocent American citizens changed the way we view liberty.

> As former Secretary of State Condoleezza Rice said at the Heritage Foundation in April 2012:
> "After 9/11, we confronted the fact that it was failed states and ungoverned spaces, and the potential nexus between terrorism and weapons of mass destruction, that threatened our very country. The fact that a stateless group of terrorists had come from a failed state—one of the poorest countries in the world, Afghanistan—to attack us and bring down the Twin Towers and blow a hole in the Pentagon. Perhaps they were paid $300,000 to do it. After that, your perception of physical security is never quite the same."[35]

Americans' immediate reaction was exceptional. From the first response of those in New York City who sacrificed their personal safety to rescue

---

[35] http://blog.heritage.org/2012/04/13/video-condoleezza-rice-speaks-on-american-exceptionalism-at-heritage/

victims trapped in the debris of the fallen towers, to the nationwide reaction to put partisan politics aside and support a president who was elected not by a majority of voters but by a 5-4 majority of the Supreme Court, Americans came together to once again exhibit the values that make us exceptional.

In the months and years that followed, however, we have lost sight of some of those values. To their credit, our government leaders sent troops into Afghanistan to stop al-Qaida and the Taliban, the extremist groups that plotted and carried out the attacks. But we also invaded and occupied a sovereign country, Iraq, based on circumstantial evidence (later proved wrong) that its government, too, participated in planning the attacks and held weapons of mass destruction that could be used to harm the United States, the United Kingdom, and our allies. Millions of innocent lives, including those of Americans, were lost as a result of this misguided military action.

Our government also used the 9/11 attacks to justify acts for which we had previously prosecuted leaders of rogue nations—torture and indefinite detention of prisoners.

In fact, our government and military set up temporary detention centers (and a permanent prison) in foreign countries because the acts performed there—extreme rendition (including government-sanctioned torture) and imprisonment without due process—are impermissible in the United States. In effect, our government rationalized the authorization of these illegal acts by having them performed elsewhere, as if that makes them acceptable or less heinous.

Of course, the question of torture is not a simple one.

Proponents have justified its use by the "ticking time bomb" scenario, where it is assumed a prisoner has knowledge that, if divulged, could save innocent lives. In this extreme instance, some say, torture can be justified.

Opponents point out that such a scenario has never actually occurred, and that the use of torture does not guarantee the receipt of accurate or truthful information.

The larger picture, it seems, is ignored.

Why would someone (or some group) want to crash commercial jets into buildings containing thousands of innocent civilians? Why would someone want to set off a bomb in Times Square?

Is it because they "hate freedom"—the superficial, bumper-sticker answer that nonetheless convinced millions of Americans to support torture?

Is it because their religion calls for the destruction of the West? Many politicians have ridden this horse to victory even though the sacred texts of Islam call for peace among peace-loving people.

Could US military intervention in other parts of the world be one motive, as suggested by US Rep. Ron Paul during the Republican Presidential Debate in South Carolina? Would the capture, torture, and indefinite detention of your son, brother, father, or other loved one make you less inclined to seek revenge, or more so? In other words: If someone treated you the same way we have, at times, treated others, would you be motivated to act out of love or out of hate?

Some Examples

Convicted terrorist Ahmed Ghailani will spend the rest of his life in prison.

Ghailani was convicted in federal criminal court in New York for his role in the 1998 bombings of US embassies in East Africa. The terrorist attacks in Nairobi, Kenya, and Tanzania killed 224 people, including twelve Americans. Ghailani was arrested in 2004 in Pakistan and held by the CIA at a secret overseas camp. He was transferred to Guantanamo Bay detention center in Cuba in 2006.

As White House then-press secretary Robert Gibbs said, the verdict "incapacitated somebody that has committed a terrorist act and because of that incapacitation is not going to threaten American lives" in the future.

But, if you listened to some Republican lawmakers, Fox News, The Weekly Standard or other conservatives, you would think Ghailani will be walking free among us. Indeed, the day after the guilty verdict was returned, most of the headlines emphasized Ghailani's acquittal on more than 280 other charges.

"I am disgusted at the total miscarriage of justice today in Manhattan's federal civilian court," said US Rep. Peter King, R-N.Y. "This tragic verdict demonstrates the absolute insanity of the Obama administration's decision to try al-Qaida terrorists in civilian courts."

"The acquittal is seen as a major blow to the US government, as Ghailani was the first former Gitmo detainee to be tried in a civilian courtroom," Fox News reported. It did not say who sees the guilty verdict as a major blow.

The Fox News story eventually mentioned that US District Judge Lewis Kaplan ruled that the prosecution's star witness would not be allowed to testify because the witness identified Ghailani while being held at a secret overseas CIA "black site" that used "harsh interrogation techniques."

"It is unknown what effect this witness would have had on the case," Fox said.

The Fox story does not specify what those "harsh interrogation techniques" were or who authorized them, nor does it note that the witness would also have been disqualified from testifying in a military tribunal had the Obama administration chosen to prosecute Ghailani there.

Nor does the Fox News story mention that there were no security breaches during the trial; that Ghailani did not use the trial to spout anti-American propaganda; and the trial did not prompt terrorist attacks in New York, as critics of the decision to try Ghailani in civilian courts claimed would happen.

The bottom line is this: A terrorist was convicted and will spend the rest of his life in prison. He was convicted in an open trial where the whole world could watch. And the government obtained justice in spite of the fact that the previous administration, by use of inhumane (and probably illegal) interrogation techniques, handcuffed the prosecution. The verdict once again confirmed the American belief in justice and due process.

One headline on the Internet: "US 1, al-Qaida 280."

More accurate: "US 1, al-Qaida 0."

US Attorney General Eric Holder's initial decision to try alleged 9/11 planner Khalid Sheikh Mohammed and his conspirators in federal court in New York rather than by military tribunal made sense for a number of reasons.

The crimes for which prosecutors believe KSM and others are responsible are the especially heinous, cold-blooded, premeditated murders of nearly three thousand innocent victims in lower Manhattan, in our nation's capital and in a field in rural Pennsylvania. The victims were for the most part not military personnel participating in the defense of our nation in a time of war, but rather ordinary citizens going about their daily business.

The weapons were not military-issued artillery or bombs strapped to the body, the preferred weapons of suicide attacks. The weapons used to kill the victims were commercial US airliners.

In other words, these were not the acts of soldiers at war. These were heinous crimes against innocent civilians. Those victims deserve justice and the perpetrators deserve the most severe punishment under the law.

It is unfortunate that Holder changed his mind about criminal trials in March 2011, after Congress refused to appropriate funds to incarcerate the defendants in New York City.

Holder's critics claimed civilian trials would grant the accused constitutional rights not afforded to foreigners. But the Founders held this truth to be self-evident: that *all* men are created equal. Not just Americans, but all men deserve due process and justice.

What were the chances that a trial would result in acquittal? Slim to none. Holder would not have brought the cases to trial if he were not confident the evidence would lead to conviction. Holder's critics declined to discuss the fact that, under military law, murder is often justifiable. Conversely, in civilian court, a defense that the murder of nearly three thousand random civilians was justifiable would likely hold no water. Holder's critics also conveniently failed to mention that military tribunals would severely condemn the waterboarding to which CIA personnel subjected KSM and others.

Many who criticized the decision to try KSM and others in a civilian court failed to see the big picture: Extremists like KSM and others don't attack the West without reason—however flawed the reason may be. They have been led to believe the United States and our allies are out to destroy Islam and the Muslim way of life.

By granting KSM and other alleged terrorists trials in civilian courts, Holder was showing the world that the United States refuses to let fanatical extremists destroy the principles on which our nation was founded and which make it the greatest country in the history of the world.

> As Secretary Rice said in her speech to the Heritage Foundation:
> "It's a pretty big agenda to react to this changing world that has undergone these shocks. And there are those who ask can we handle this challenge and still pursue our values? I suggest we can handle this challenge *only if we pursue our values.*"[36] (My emphasis)

In other words: America is exceptional not because it is America, but because of the principles and values it holds sacred. When we stray from

---

[36]   Ibid.

those values (invading a sovereign nation in retribution for an attack it had nothing to do with, for example, resulting in tens of thousands of innocent civilian deaths), America fails. But, if we acknowledge our failure, sincerely apologize and take steps to ensure it won't happen again, we can restore our country to its place of honor and respect.

If we let the terrorists change our values, the terrorists win.